Thos Kingsford

1809

THE

RULE of LIFE.

[Price 3s.]

THE

RULE of LIFE,

IN

SELECT SENTENCES:

COLLECTED

FROM THE GREATEST AUTHORS,

ANCIENT and MODERN.

Know Thyself. DEL. ORAC.

THE ELEVENTH EDITION, CORRECTED,

WITH ADDITIONS.

LONDON:

PRINTED FOR W. BENT, PATER NOSTER ROW.

MDCCXCIV.

PREFACE.

THE greatest ornament of the ac-
complished gentleman, is his perfect
knowledge of things, and deep inspection
into the principal characters of men.
He that aims at this knowledge, says the
learned Gracian, must make a collection
of all good thoughts in books; of apoph-
thegms, or heroical expressions, wise mens
axioms, and observations, &c.   Now,
the laying together these necessary ma-
terials, as a foundation, is the work of
the following sheets; but the superstruc-
ture must be the reader's part, and can
only be perfected by himself; that is, by
application and practice.

A 3   Pre-

Precepts, *when contracted into sentences, strike the affections, and are more easily retained: and a few useful ones at hand (according to* Seneca*) do more toward a* happy life, *than whole volumes of cautions, that we know not where to find.*

Of the variety of books of this nature, that are published, few answer the design, and most of them are filled with low and trivial matter, that affords little instruction or improvement; yet, as some good things are interspersed among them, those I have here transplanted; and acknowledge these papers to be so far enriched by them: but the major part is extracted from the writings of the most eminent Philosophers, Divines, *and* Moralists, *and other approved* Authors, *that have written in the* sententious *way.*

My

My endeavonr has been to follow nature, *and keep cloſe to* truth. *What
ſeemed to be abſtruſe, is made clear; and
what prolix, contracted in as few words
as poſſible, not to loſe their ſtrength and
beauty.   It cannot be expected, that
every ſentence ſhould have the authority
of a* maxim: *ſtars differ in brightneſs;
yet thoſe that ſhine the leaſt may have
their influence.*

*It was neither practicable, nor did I
think it neceſſary, to clog every line, or
ſentence, with* citation; *for what is
good, will ſtand ſo, without any great
name to ſupport it: but as ſome are curious
of knowing who ſpeaks, as well as what
is ſaid, I have to ſeveral paſſages mentioned from whence they were taken.*

The whole is a picture of human
life, *wherein the* paſſions, follies, *and*
2   foibles

foibles *of mankind are delineated, and expressed in their proper colours:* virtue *is set forth in the most amiable light, and* vice *exposed in its natural deformity.*

A compendium of moral institutes and counsels, drawn from the best writers, will be always entertaining to ingenious minds. And, to make reading the more agreeable, the greatest part is digested under proper heads; the rest are miscellaneous: every page containing such variety of useful reflections, as to yield at once both profit and pleasure.

THE

THE

CONTENTS.

Of

x   The CONTENTS.

Coun-

THE

THE

RULE OF LIFE.

OF EDUCATION, GENIUS, PRECEPT, AND EXAMPLE.

THE great bufinefs of a man is to improve his mind and govern his manners. *Antoninus.*

The educator's care, above all things fhould be, firft, to lay in his charge the foundation of religion and virtue.

What fculpture is to a block of marble, education is to a human foul. The philofopher, the faint, and the hero, the wife, the good, or the great man, very often lie hid and concealed in a plebeian, which a proper education might have difinterred, and have brought to light. *Spec.*

If we inquire after the caufe, that men grow every day more loofe in their princi-

B   ciples,

ciples, and vicious in their practices, it seems to be, that, in the places of education of persons of all ranks, there is no book taught that has any relation to the *sacred writings*.

Parents are commonly more careful to bestow wit on their children, than virtue; the art of speaking well, rather than doing well: but their manners ought to be the great concern.

It ought always to be steadily inculcated, that virtue is the highest proof of understanding, and the only solid basis of greatness; and that vice is the natural consequence of narrow thoughts; that it begins in mistake, and ends in ignominy.   *Johnson.*

That man must have a strange value for words, when he can think it worth while to hazard the innocence and virtue of his son, for a little Greek and Latin; while he should be laying the solid foundations of knowledge in his mind, and furnishing it with just rules to direct his future progress in life.   *Locke.*

The subject of duties is the most useful part of all philosophy.   *Cicero.*

To be prudent, honest, and good, are infinitely higher accomplishments, than the being

being nice, florid, learned, or all that which the world calls great scholars, and fine gentlemen. *Charron.*

An induſtrious and virtuous education of children is a better inheritance for them, than a great eſtate. To what purpoſe is it, ſaid *Crates*, to heap up great eſtates, and have no concern what manner of heirs you leave them to ?

A falſe ſtep in the inſtitution is as much many times, as ſoul, body, and eſtate, are worth.

Ageſilaus, being aſked, what he thought moſt proper for boys to learn; anſwered, what they ought to do when they come to be men.

Philoſophy, ſays *Seneca*, is turned to philology, and through the fault of both maſters and ſcholars: *they* teach to diſpute, not to live; and *theſe* come to them to mend their wits, not their manners.

There is in ſome tempers ſuch a natural barrenneſs, that, like the ſands of Arabia, they are never to be cultivated or improved. And ſome will never learn any thing becauſe they underſtand every thing too ſoon.

There is no ſuch fop as my young maſter, who is a fool of his lady mother's making:

ſhe

fhe blows him up into a conceit of himfelf, and there he ftops, without ever advancing one ftep further: fhe makes a man of him at fixteen, and a boy all the days of his life after. *Spec.*

Many of our young gentlemen, who are fent abroad, bring home, inftead of folid virtue, formalities, fafhions, grimaces, and at beft a volubility of talking nonfenfe; yet fome perhaps think them well educated; and that foreign vanity is preferable to home difcretion.

The proverb fays, *the fpirit of a fitting man is moft prudent.* Thofe who are naturally deftitute of judgment and prudence, become greater fools by their *travelling*; it being impoffible for him, who is a fool in his own country, to become wife by running up and down. Which made *Socrates* fay, he muft change his fpirit, and not his climate, to become wife.

Zeno, hearing a young man fpeak too freely, told him, for this reafon we have two ears, and but one tongue; that we fhould hear much and fpeak little.

Xenophon commended the Perfians for the prudent education of their children, who would not permit them to effeminate their minds

minds with amorous ftories, and idle romances, being fufficiently convinced of the danger of adding weight to the bias of corrupt nature.

Emulation is a great incitement to induftry. *Quintilian*, among his excellent rules for inftructing of youth, fpeaks to this purpofe: give me a child that is fenfible of praife, and touched with glory, and that will cry at the fhame of being outdone; and I will keep him to his bufinefs by *emulation:* reproof will afflict, and honour will encourage him, and I fhall not fear to cure him of his idlenefs.

The magifterial feverity of fome pedagogues frights more learning out of children, than ever they can whip into them.

None can be eminent without application and genius. *Ariftotle* fays, that to become an able man in any profeffion whatfoever, three things are neceffary, which are *nature*, *ftudy*, and *practice.*

A man of ingenuity may go a great way in the field of learning, by himfelf. *Heraclitus*, a philofopher of Ephefus, had no mafter or tutor; but attained to great knowledge by his own private ftudy and diligence. Though this can be no rule,

it

it is an example to thofe who have not the advantage of a guide.

Phocylides, the Greek poet, likened education to a fickle and a hand, for this reafon; if there was any vice in the foul, it would weed it out; and, if there was no virtue as yet in the foul, it would plant fome in.

The memory of the ancients is hardly in any thing more to be celebrated, than in their ftrict and ufeful inftitution of youth: by labour they prevented luxury in their young people, till wifdom and philofophy had taught them to refift and defpife it.

The bulk of mankind muft, without the affiftance of education and inftruction, be informed only with the underftanding of a child. *Johnfon*.

It is obferved, that education is generally the worfe, in proportion to the wealth and grandeur of the parents. Many are apt to think, that to dance, fence, fpeak French, and know how to behave among great perfons, comprehends the whole duty of a gentleman; which opinion is enough to deftroy all the feeds of knowledge, honour, wifdom, and virtue among us. *Swift*.

Lycurgus

Lycurgus feeing a keeper teaching a bloodhound to follow a train; obferve, faid he, what pains yonder mafter takes to make his fervant ufeful and profitable for his pleafure : who would not then train up with diligence his fon in the fchool of virtue, that he may be a profitable fervant of the commonwealth ?

He that is taught to live upon little, owes more to his father's wifdom, than he that has a great deal left him, does to his father's care.

It is great imprudence to determine children to any particular bufinefs, before their temper and inclinations are well known. Every one, fays *Horace*, is beft in his own profeffion ; that which fits us beft, is beft ; nor is any thing more fitting, than that every one fhould confider his own genius and capacity, and act accordingly.

The mind ought fometimes to be diverted, that it may return to thinking the better. Little reading, and much thinking, little fpeaking, and much hearing, is the beft way to improve in knowledge.

Our common education is not intended to render us good and wife, but learned : it has not taught us to follow and embrace virtue and prudence, but has imprinted in us their derivation and etymology; it has chofen out for us, not fuch books as contain the foundeft and trueft opinions, but thofe that fpeak the beft Greek and Latin; and by thefe rules has inftilled into our fancy the vaineft humours of antiquity. But a good education alters the judgment and manners. *Ful.*

The fciences chiefly to be recommended are natural and moral philofophy; for thefe entertain us with the images and beauties both of nature and of virtue; fhow us what we are, and what we ought to be: to which we may add mechanics, agriculture, and navigation. Moft other ftudies are, in a manner, emptinefs and air; diverfions to re-create the mind, but not of weight enough to make them our bufinefs. *Charron.*

The end of learning is to know GOD, and out of that knowledge to love him, and to imitate him, as we may the neareft by poffeffing our fouls of true virtue. *Milton.*

Of CUSTOM, NOVELTY, and OPINION.

IT is the common cuſtom of the world to follow example, rather than precept; but it would be the ſafer courſe to learn by precept, rather than example.

Many bad things are done only for cuſtom; which will make a *good* practice as eaſy to us as an *ill* one.

Examples do not authorize a fault. Vice muſt never plead preſcription.

Cuſtom is the plague of wiſe men, and the idol of fools.

Moſt men live according to opinion or faſhion, which is full of variety, and therefore of perturbation; leaving the direct rule of wiſdom, which renders us calm and ſerene.

Cuſtom ſurpaſſes nature, eſpecially in vice and diſſoluteneſs. When young men know, that they have an unbridled licence, all hope of amendment is utterly periſhed in them, and it is next to impoſſible to reclaim them by counſel, inſtruction, or reaſon.

B 5   The

The opinions of men are as many and as different as their perfons; the greateft diligence, and moft prudent conduct, can never pleafe them all.

Cuftom leffens admiration. An indifferent novelty commonly carries it from the higheft excellence that begins to grow old.

It was a good reply of *Plato*, to one who murmured at his reproving him for a fmall matter: *cuftom*, faid he, *is no fmall matter*. A cuftom or habit of life does frequently alter the natural inclination either to good or evil.

It is common, fays *Tacitus*, to efteem moft what is moft unknown.

Nature has been extremely fruitful of wonders in thefe kingdoms, that compofe the Britifh monarchy; and it is a ridiculous cuftom, that gentlemen of fortune fhould be carried away with a defire of feeing the curiofities of other countries, before they have any tolerable infight into their own. Travelling fometimes makes a wife man better, but always a fool worfe.

Opinion is the main thing which does good or harm in the world. It is our falfe opinions of things which ruin us.

Whether

Whether fondnefs of fafhion, or love of novelty, betray men into the moft miftakes, it is difficult to determine. The beft things are flighted by fome for mere antiquity, though founded upon authority and reafon; and others maintain a veneration for whatever cuftom has eftablifhed, though founded upon neither.

Every novelty appears more wonderful, as it is more remote from any thing with which experience or teftimony have hitherto acquainted us; and if it paffes further beyond the notions that we have been accuftomed to form, it becomes at laft incredible. *Johnfon.*

Opinion is the guide of fools; but wife men are conducted by reafon and prudence: it is a monfter; half truth, and half falfehood.

The moft barren ground, by manuring, may be made to produce good fruit; the fierceft beafts, by art, are made tame; fo are moral virtues acquired by cuftom. *Plut.*

Vicious habits are fo great a ftain to human nature, and fo odious in themfelves, that every perfon, actuated by right reafon, would avoid them, though he was fure they would be always concealed both from God

and.

and man, and had no future punifhment entailed upon them. *Cicero.*

Moft men judge according to their interefts, and abound in their own fenfe. Let two be of a contrary opinion, yet each prefumes to have right on his fide: but reafon, that has always been faithful, never had two faces. *Gracian.*

Much of the pain and pleafure of mankind arifes from the conjectures which every one makes of the thoughts of others. We all enjoy praife which we do not hear, and refent contempt which we do not fee. *Johnfon.*

Novelty has charms, that our minds can hardly withftand. The moft valuable things, if they have for a long while appeared among us, do not make any impreffion as they are good, but give us diftafte as they are old. But, when the influence of this fantaftical humour is over, the fame men or things will come to be admired again, by a happy return of our good tafte. *St. Evremond.*

OF

Of LAW, JUSTICE, INJURY, and OPPRESSION.

AS to be perfectly juſt is an attribute of the Divine Nature; to be ſo, to the utmoſt of our abilities, is the glory of a man. *Addiſ.*

No man is wiſe or ſafe, but he that is honeſt. *Raleigh.*

Judges ought to be more learned than witty, more reverend than plauſible, and more adviſed than confident: above all things, integrity is their portion, and proper virtue. *Bacon.*

Of all injuſtice, that is the greateſt which goes under the name of law; and, of all ſorts of tyranny, the forcing of the *letter* of the law againſt the *equity* is the moſt inſupportable. *L'Eſtr.*

Juſtice, without mercy, is extreme injury; and it is as great tyranny, not to mitigate laws, as iniquity to break them. The extremity of right is extremity of wrong.

Equity judgeth with lenity, laws with extremity. In all moral caſes, the *reaſon* of the law, is the law. *Scott.*

When

When *Auguſtus* was to give ſentence upon a ſon, who would have killed his father, he did not, as the law required, command him to be thrown into the Tyber, but only to be baniſhed whither his father pleaſed; remembering, that although the ſon deſerved the worſt, yet fathers love to inflict the leaſt.

He that paſſes a ſentence haſtily, looks as if he did it willingly; and there is an injuſtice in the exceſs. *Sen.*

A judge, who is prepoſſeſſed in any cauſe, and does not hear both ſides indifferently, though the judgment he gives be right, yet himſelf errs; for there can be no integrity, where there is any partiality.

Alexander, when he heard any one accuſed, would ſtop one ear with his hand, thereby reſerving audience for the defendant.

Our law ſays well, *to delay juſtice is injuſtice.* Not to have a right, and not to come at it, differ little.

Innocence is no protection againſt tyrannical power; for accuſing is proving, where malice and force are joined in the proſecution. Force governs the world, and ſucceſs conſecrates the cauſe. What avails it

2　　　　　the

the lamb to have the better caufe, if the wolf have the ftronger teeth? It is to no purpofe to ftand reafoning, where the adverfary is both party and judge.

Cicero complained, that many worthy ordinances were fettled by laws; but thofe, for the moft part, were corrupted and depraved by lawyers inventions.

At Thebes were erected ftatues of judges having no hands, and the chief of them had his eyes fhut; thereby fignifying, that among them juftice was not to be folicited either with bribery or addrefs.

All the laws, both of God and man, fuffer fuch actions as are done involuntarily to go unpunifhed.

Where no law is, there is no tranfgreffion.

He that is not above an injury, is below himfelf.

It is a univerfally acknowledged maxim, that as foon as any contracting party departs from the condition of his engagements, the other is no longer bound by his.

Magiftrates are to obey, as well as execute laws. Power is not to do wrong, but to punifh the doers of wrong.

Archidamus

Archidamus being afked, who was the mafter of Sparta; anfwered, the laws, and next them the magiftrates.

Religion in a magiftrate ftrengthens his authority, becaufe it procures veneration, and gains a reputation to it: and, in all the affairs of this world, fo much reputation is really fo much power.　*Tillotf.*

Nothing is more againft reafon and nature, than for a man to exact of his neighbour beyond his ability, or opprefs him by violence and force, or colour of law: it is enough for fuch to bear their misfortune, without being perfecuted, and treated with that infolence and feverity they too often meet with.　Lawful ends may be very unlawfully attained.

Neceffity, that great refuge and excufe for human frailty, breaks through all laws; and he is not to be accounted in fault, whofe crime is not the effect of choice, but force.　*Sen.*

The man who wants mercy, makes the law of the land his gofpel, and all his cafes of confcience are determined by his attorney.　The guilt of being unfortunate is never to be defended by the beft advocate in the world; all he can do, or fay, will be

received

received with prejudice by an uncompaf-
fionate creditor. *Spec.*

Solon being afked, why among his laws,
there was not one againft perfonal affronts;
anfwered, he could not believe the world
fo fantaftical as to regard them.

A promife againft law or duty is void in
its own nature. If it be juft, fays *Agefilaus*,
I promifed it; if unjuft, I only faid it.
And that is the condition of the obligations
in all cafes.

It was the faying of a certain prince,
that we muft difpenfe with juftice in fmall
matters to keep it in greater.

There have been many laws made by
men, which fwerve from honefty, reafon,
and the dictates of nature. By the *law of
arms*, he his degraded from all honour who
puts up an affront; and, by the *civil law*,
he that takes vengeance for it, incurs a ca-
pital punifhment. He that feeks redrefs
by law for an affront, is difgraced; and he
that does not feek redrefs this way, is punifhed by the laws. *Montaigne.*

Fidelity and truth are the foundation of
all juftice.

Perjury is not only a wrong to particular
perfons, but treafon againft human fociety;
fub-

subverting at once the foundations of public peace and justice, and the private security of every man's life and fortune. *Tillotf.*

In this world men thrive by villainy; and lying and deceiving are accounted just, and to be rich is to be wife, and tyranny is honorable; and though little thefts and petty mischiefs are interrupted by the laws, yet if a mischief become public and great, acted by princes, and effected by armies, and robberies be done by whole fleets, it is virtue, and it is glory. *Taylor.*

If every fuitor suffered as much for the holy faith, as he does about the travel of his procefs, there would be as many martyrs in chancery, and other courts of justice, as were at Rome in the times of persecutions by the old emperors.

The laws keep up their credit, not because they are all just, but because they are laws: this is the myftical foundation of their authority, and they have no other. *Montaigne.*

OF

Of TEMPERANCE, PRUDENCE, and FORTITUDE.

THE richeſt endowments of the mind are temperance, prudence, and fortitude. Prudence is a univerſal virtue, which enters into the compoſition of all the reſt; and where that is not, fortitude loſes its name and nature. *Voiture.*

Self-denial is the moſt exalted pleaſure; and the conqueſt of evil habits is the moſt glorious triumph.

A wiſe man ſtands firm in all extremities, and bears the lot of his humanity with a divine temper. *Sen.*

What can be more honorable than to have courage enough to execute the commands of reaſon and conſcience; to maintain the dignity of our nature, and the ſtation aſſigned us: to be proof againſt poverty, pain, and death itſelf; ſo far as not to do any thing that is ſcandalous or ſinful to avoid them: to ſtand adverſity under all ſhapes with decency and reſolution? To do this is to be great above title and fortune. This argues the ſoul of a heavenly

extrac-

extraction, and is worthy the offspring of the Deity. *Col.*

Virtue is made for difficulties, and grows stronger and brighter for such trials.

Men will have the same veneration for a person who suffers adversity without dejection, as for demolished temples, the very ruins whereof are reverenced and adored.

There is an heroic innocence as well as an heroic courage. *St. Evr.*

It is a maxim of prudence, to leave things before they leave us.

The true way to advance another's virtue, is to follow it; and the best means to cry down another's vice, is to decline it.

There can be no peace in human life without the contempt of all events. *Sen.*

The greater the difficulty, the more glory in surmounting it; skilful pilots gain their reputation from storms and tempests.

To be valorous is not always to be venturous.

As fortitude suffers not the mind to be dejected with any evils; so temperance suffers it not to be drawn from honesty by any allurements.

A warm

A warm heart requires a cool head. Courage without conduct is like fancy without judgment; all fail and no ballaft.

No man was ever caft down with the injuries of fortune, but he fuffered himfelf before to be deceived by her favours.

Judgment is the throne of prudence, and filence is its fanctuary.

Nothing would fortify us more againft any manner of accidents, than the poffeffing our fouls with this maxim; *we can never be hurt but by ourfelves.* If our reafon be what it ought, and our actions according to it, we are invulnerable. *Char.*

Fortitude has its extremes, as well as the reft of the virtues; and ought, like them, to be always attended by prudence. *Voiture.*

A wife man is out of the reach of fortune, and all attempts upon him are no more than *Xerxes'* arrows; they may darken the day, but they cannot ftrike the fun.

Charity obliges not to miftruft a man; prudence, not to truft him before we know him.

He who lofes wealth lofes much; he who lofes a friend, lofes more; but he that lofes his fpirits, lofes all.

A virtuous

A virtuous and well-difpofed perfon, like to good metal, the more he is fired, the more he is fined; the more he is oppofed, the more he is approved: wrongs may well try him, and touch him, but cannot imprint in him any falfe ftamp. *Rich.*

The virtue of *profperity* is temperance; the virtue of *adverfity* is fortitude; which in morals is the more heroical virtue. Profperity is the bleffing of the Old Teftament, adverfity is ths bleffing of the New, which carries the greater benediction, and the clearer revelation of God's favour. *Bacon.*

Though fortune feems to be a univerfal miftrefs, yet prudence belongs to her. When we are guided by prudence, we are furrounded by all other divinities.

Prudence is of more frequent ufe than any other intellectual quality; it is exerted on flight occafions, and called into act by the curfory bufinefs of common life. *Johnfon.*

There is a mean in all things: even virtue itfelf has its ftated limits; which not being ftrictly obferved, it ceafes to be virtue. *Horace.*

A virtuous habit of the mind is fo abfolutely neceffary to influence the whole life, and beautify every particular action; to over-balance or repel all the gilded charms of avarice, pride, and felf-intereft; that a man defervedly procures the lafting epithets of *good* or *bad*, as he appears either fwayed by, or regardlefs of it.

The prerogatives of good men appear plainly in this; that men bear more honour to the fepulchres of the virtuous, than to the palaces of the wicked.

A man of virtue is a honour to his country, a glory to humanity, and fatisfaction to himfelf, and a benefactor to the whole world: he is rich without oppreffion or difhonefty, charitable without oftentation, courteous without deceit, and brave without vice.

Of

Of ANGER and REVENGE.

AN angry man, who suppresses his passions, thinks worse than he speaks; and an angry man that will chide, speaks worse than he thinks. *Bacon.*

If you be affronted, it is better to pass it by in silence, or with a jest, though with some dishonour, than to endeavour revenge. If you can keep reason above passion, that and watchfulness will be your best defendants. *Newton.*

Better to prevent a quarrel beforehand, than to revenge it afterward.

A vindictive temper is not only uneasy to others, but to them that have it.

Dislike what deserves it, but never hate; for that is of the nature of malice, which is almost ever to persons, not to things.

Anger may glance into the breast of a wise man, but rests only in the bosom of fools.

In all things, mistakes are excusable; but an error that proceeds from any good principle, leaves no room for resentment.

None

None more impatiently suffer injuries, than those that are most forward in doing them.

What men want of reason for their opinions, they usually supply and make up in rage. *Tillotf.*

It was a good method observed by *Socrates:* when he found in himself any disposition to anger, he would check it by speaking *low*, in opposition to the motions of his displeasure.

Discord is every-where a troublesome companion : but when it is shut up within a family, and happens among relations that cannot easily part, it is harder to deal with.

It is much better to reprove than to be angry secretly.

He that waits for an opportunity of acting his revenge, watches to do himself a mischief.

Passion evaporates by words, as grief does by tears.

By taking revenge, a man is but even with his enemy ; but, in passing it over, he is superior. *Bacon.*

C							It

It is the only valour, to remit a wrong; and the greatest applause, that I may hurt, and would not.

To be able to bear provocation is an argument of great wisdom; and to forgive it, of a great mind. *Tillotf.*

It costs more to revenge injuries, than to bear them.

One long anger, and twenty short ones, have no very great difference.

He that will be angry for any thing, will be angry for nothing.

The most irreconcileable enmities grow from the most intimate friendships.

None should be so implacable as to refuse a humble submission. He whose very best actions must be seen with favorable allowance, cannot be too mild, moderate, and forgiving. *Spec.*

To pardon faults of error is but justice to the failings of our nature.

There cannot possibly be a greater extravagance, than for a man to run the hazard of losing his life to satisfy his revenge. When *Mark Anthony*, after the battle of Actium, challenged *Augustus*, he took no further notice of the insult, than sending

back

back this anfwer: If Anthony was weary of his life, there were other ways of difpatch befide fighting him; and, for his part, he fhould not trouble himfelf to be his executioner.

The nobleft remedy for injuries is oblivion. Light injuries are made none, by not regarding them.

To err, is human; to forgive, divine. *Pope.*

Only by pride comes contention.

Revenge ftops at nothing that is violent and wicked. The hiftories of all ages are full of the tragical outrages that have been executed by this diabolical paffion.

It was a ftrange revenge of a countryman who was the laft life in the leafe of an eftate, in his patron's poffeffion; who, taking fomewhat ill of his landlord, immediately poifoned himfelf, to defeat the other of the eftate.

A more glorious victory cannot be gained over another man, than this: that, when the injury began on his part, the kindnefs fhould begin on ours. *Tillotf.*

If we do not fubdue our anger, it will fubdue us. It is the fecond word that makes the quarrel.

C 2　　　　　　Yielding

Yielding pacifies great offences.

We ought to divest ourselves of hatred, for the interest of our own quiet. *St Evr.*

Anger begins with folly, and ends with repentance. *Pythag.*

We often forgive those that have injured us; but we can never pardon those that we have injured. *Rochef.*

The more high and lofty a building is, the more props it wants to be kept up. We ought never to despise the resentment of our inferiors, because the less we fear it, the more it is dangerous.

As we often are incensed without cause, so we continue our anger, lest it should appear to our disgrace, to have begun without occasion.

A wise man has no more anger than shows he can apprehend the *first* wrong, nor any more revenge than justly to prevent a *second.*

Vexation is rather taken than given. Revenge never repairs an injury.

Hipponax, a poet of Ephesus, was so deformed of visage, that *Bupalus* drew his picture for men to laugh at: upon which he wrote such sharp verses against the paint-

er,

er, that for anger and fhame he hanged himfelf.

A man does then only take fatisfaction and revenge, when he humbles his enemy, and forces him to fubmiffion. *Char.*

One unquiet perverfe difpofition diftempers the peace and unity of a whole family or fociety; as one jarring inftrument will fpoil a whole concert.

Our paffions are like the feas agitated by the winds; and as GOD has fet bounds to thofe, fo fhould we to thefe: *fo far they fhall go, and no farther.*

In ficknefs, our diftemper make us loathe the moft natural meat; in anger, our fury makes us refift the moft courteous advice.

That anger is not warrantable that has feen two funs.

The moft tolerable fort of revenge is for thofe wrongs which there is no law to remedy: but then let a man take heed that the revenge be fuch as there is no law to punifh; elfe a man's enemy is ftill beforehand, and is two for one. *Bacon.*

There is not any revenge more heroic, than that which torments envy, by doing good.

Diogenes

Diogenes, being afked, how one fhould be revenged of his enemy; anfwered, by being a virtuous and honeft man.

The difcretion of a man defers his anger, and it is glory to pafs over a tranfgreffion.

It was a pretty victory which *Euclid* got of his angry brother, who, being highly difpleafed, cried out, *let me perifh, if I le not revenged!* But he anfwered, *and let me perifh, if I do not make you kind, and quickly to forget your anger!*

Men of proud and paffionate tempers, like thofe who have peftilential difeafes, have only this advantage from their defects, that, though they be not guilty at all of valour, yet they caufe all the world to fly from them.   *Balzac.*

Inconfiderate rafhnefs may leffen the evil of a mifchance done by us, but cannot fully abfolve us from it.   For reafon is given us, that in all our actions we fhould govern ourfelves by advice of it.

We muft forget the good we do, for fear of upbraiding: and religion bids us forget injuries, left the remembrance of them fhould fuggeft to us a defire of revenge.

Hatred

Hatred is ſo durable and ſo obſtinate, that reconciliation on a ſickbed is the greateſt ſign of death. *Bruyere.*

A paſſionate temper renders a man unfit for advice, deprives him of his reaſon, robs him of all that is great or noble in his nature; it makes him unfit for converſation, deſtroys friendſhip, changes juſtice into cruelty, and turns all order into confuſion.

Thoſe who are vexed to impatience, are angry to ſee others leſs diſturbed than themſelves; but when others begin to rave, they immediately ſee in them what they could not find in themſelves, the deformity and folly of uſeleſs rage.

Of

Of AMBITION, AVARICE, PRIDE, and PRODIGALITY.

OF all human actions, pride feldomeft obtains its end; for aiming at honour and reputation, it reaps contempt and derifion.

Covetous men need money leaft, yet moft affect it; and prodigals, who need it moft, do leaft regard it.

That plenty fhould produce either covetoufnefs or prodigality, is a perverfion of providence; and yet the generality of men are the worfe for their riches.

Poverty wants fome, luxury many, avarice all things. *Cowley.*

To live above our ftation fhows a proud heart; and to live under it difcovers a narrow foul.

There is no greater fign of a mean and fordid fpirit than to doat upon riches; nor is any thing more magnificent than to lay them out freely in acts of bounty and liberality. *Cicero.*

Avarice and ambition are the two elements that enter into the compofition of all crimes.

crimes. Ambition is boundlefs, and avarice infatiable.

Sordid felfifhnefs does contract and narrow our benevolence, and caufe us, like ferpents, to unfold ourfelves within ourfelves, and turn out our ftings to all the world befide. *Scott.*

Pride and illnature will be hated in fpite of all the wealth and greatnefs in the world. Civility is always fafe; but pride creates us enemies.

If a proud man makes me keep my diftance, the comfort is, he keeps his at the fame time. *Swift.*

Where avarice rules, there is nothing of humanity. Intereft fuperfedes all arguments of affection and confanguinity.

Money, like dung, does no good till it is fpread. There is no real ufe of riches, except it be in the diftribution; the reft is but conceit. *Bacon.*

Some are by nature fo covetous and miferable, that it is as much in vain to attempt to enlarge their minds, as to go about to plough the rocks.

Liberality makes friends of enemies; but pride makes enemies of friends.

it

It is fruition, and not poffeffion, that renders us happy. *Montaigne.*

Oftentation and pride, upon the account cf honours and preferments, is much more offenfive, than upon any perfonal qualifications. *Roihef.*

It is not the *height* to which men are advanced, that makes them giddy; it is the *looking down* with contempt upon thofe below them.

A *cavalier*, hearing that an old friend of his was advanced to a *cardinalate*, went to congratulate his eminence upon his new honour. —Pray, fir, fays the *cardinal*, may I crave the favour of your name, and your bufinefs? I am come, fays the *cavalier*, to condole with your eminence, and to tell you how heartily I pity men that are overcharged with dignity and preferment; for it turns fome people's brains to that degree, that they can neither fee nor hear, nor underftand, like other men; and makes them as abfolutely to forget their old friends, as if they had never feen them before in their lives.

Seneca obferves well, that it is the conftant fault, and infeparable ill quality of ambition, never to look behind it.

It is a very great unhappinefs in a man to be too well known to the world, and too much unknown to himfelf. *Alexander* was below a man, when he affected to be a god.

The fame action which has no lefs than a diadem for its aim, has often an igno-minious death for its end.

He has moft that covets leaft. A wife man (fays fir *P. Sidney*) wants but little, becaufe he defires not much.

It is rightly faid, that covetoufnefs muft be a miferable vice, to weary man in pro-curing riches, and not fuffer him to enjoy them when gotten.

What can be a more wretched fight, than to fee a ftarving mifer *mortify* without re-ligion? To fubmit to fuch voluntary hard-fhips to no purpofe, and lofe the prefent, without providing for the future?

He that fpares in every thing is nig-gardly; and he that fpares in nothing is profufe: neither of which can be generous or liberal.

The prodigal robs his heir, the mifer robs himfelf. *Bruyere.*

It is a much eafier tafk to dig metal out of its native mine, than to get it out of the

covetous

covetous man's coffer.   Death only has the key of the mifer's cheft.

He is a flave to the greateft flave, that ferves none but himfelf.

Pitiful! that a man fhould fo care for riches, as if they were his own; yet fo ufe them, as if they were another's: that when he might be happy in fpending them, will be miferable in keeping them; and had rather, dying, leave wealth with his enemies, than, being alive, relieve his friends.

Zeno faid, that an avaricious man was like barren fandy ground, which fucks in all the rain and dew with greedinefs and thirft; but yields no fruitful herbs or plants to the inhabitants.

Many take a pride to infult over the timorous; and mean and low fubmiffions do but fwell them up to a more extravagant and remorfelefs barbarity.   *Char.*

Pride joined with many virtues, chokes them all.

Some people are all quality; you would think they were made up of nothing but title and genealogy: the ftamp of dignity defaces in them the very charadter of humanity, and tranfports them to fuch a degree of haughtinefs, that they reckon it below

below them to exercife either goodnature or complaifance.

If we could trace our defcents, fays *Se-neca*, we fhould find all flaves to come from princes, and all princes from flaves. We are all of us compofed of the fame elements; all of us equal, if we could but recover our evidence: but, when we can carry it no further, the herald provides us fome hero to fupply the place of an illuftrious original; and there is the rife of arms and families.

Likenefs begets love; yet proud men hate one another.

Intereft fpeaks all manner of languages, and acts all forts of parts: virtues are loft in intereft, as rivers in the fea.

A poor fpirit is poorer than a poor purfe. A very few pounds a year would eafe a man of the fcandal of avarice. *Swift*.

What madnefs is it for a man to ftarve himfelf, to enrich his heir, and fo turn a friend into an enemy! For his joy at your death will be proportioned to what you leave him. *Seneca*.

Hiftory tells us of illuftrious villains; but there was never an illuftrious mifer in nature. *St. Evr.*

It

It is as difagreeable to a prodigal to keep an account of his expences, as it is to a finner to examine his confcience; the deeper they fearch, the worfe they find themfelves.

A wife man will defire no more than what he may get juftly, ufe foberly, diftribute cheerfully, and live contentedly. *Bacon.*

Nothing can be more vain than to court popular applaufe, if we confider the emptinefs of the found, the precarious tenure, the little judgment of thofe that give it us, and the narrow compafs it is confined to.

The beft kindnefs of a proud man has often fuch a mixture of arrogancy, as their greateft obligations are rendered ungracious to a worthy receiver.

It is rare to fee an immoderate ambition which is not accompained with a mean fubjection.

Where is that advantage under the fun, that any but a madman would be proud of? Or where is that pride itfelf, that any mortal in his right wits would not find reafon to be afhamed of? *L'Eftr.*

He that fwells in profperity, will fhrink in adverfity.

To

To be proud of knowledge is to be blind in the light; to be proud of virtue is to poison yourſelf with the antidote; to be proud of authority is to make your riſe your downfal.

There is not the greateſt man living, but may ſtand in need of the meaneſt, as much as the meaneſt does of him.

The beſt way to humble a proud man is to take no notice of him.

Ambition to rule is more vehement than malice to revenge.

The talleſt trees are moſt in the power of the winds, and ambitious men of the blaſts of fortune. Great marks are fooneſt hit.

A perſon who ſquanders away his fortune in rioting and profuſeneſs, is neither juſt to himſelf or others; for, by a conduct of this kind, his ſuperfluities flow in an irregular channel, and thoſe that are the moſt unworthy are the greateſt ſharers of them, who do not fail to cenſure him when his ſubſtance is exhauſted.

A man's deſires always diſappoint him; for, though he meets with ſomething that gives him ſatisfaction, yet it never thoroughly anſwers his expectation. *Rufo.*

If

If money be not thy servant, it will be thy master. The covetous man cannot so properly be said to possess wealth, as that may be said to possess him. *Char.*

What man in his right senses, that has wherewithal to live free, would make himself a slave for superfluities? What does that man want, who has enough? Or what is he the better for abundance, that can never be satisfied? *L'Estr.*

The only gratification a covetous man gives his neighbours, is to let them see, that he himself is as little the better for what he has, as they are.

Tantalus, it is said, was ready to perish with thirst, though up to the chin in water. Change but the name, and every rich miser is the *Tantalus* in the fable. He sits gaping over his money, and dares no more touch it than he dares to commit sacrilege.

The prodigal has as little charity in him as the miser: his flinty soul is not to be touched with any tenderness, humanity, or commiseration; neither poverty nor distress, innocence nor merit, can melt him: that noble truth in *sacred writ*, of a superior happiness in giving than in receiving, he never experienced.

Pride

Pride had rather at any time go out of the way, than come behind.

When *Darius* offered *Alexander* 10,000 talents, to divide Asia equally with him, he answered, the earth cannot bear two suns, nor Asia two kings. *Parmenio*, a friend of *Alexander*, hearing the great offers *Darius* had made, said, were I *Alexander* I would accept them: so would I, replied *Alexander*, were I *Parmenio*.

The most laudable ambition is to be wise; and the greatest wisdom is to be good. We may be as ambitious as we please, so we aspire to the best things.

Cleobulus being asked, why he sought not to be advanced to honour and preferment, made this reply: O friend, as long as I study and practise humility, I know where I am; but, when I shall hunt after dignities and promotion, I am afraid I shall loose myself.

Other vices choose to be in the dark; only pride loves always to be in the light.

Turn the carcase the wrong side outward, said the emperor *Antoninus*, and be proud, if you can; and, to improve your thought, consider what a beauty age, diseases, and death will make of you.

How

How deplorable is the blindneſs of human pride! Some muſt have their dead bodies laid in ſtate, pompous funerals, ſuperb monuments; which fills men, in a manner, with their own emptineſs; which turns the ſaddeſt warnings GOD gives them, in order to humble them, into the moſt dangerous illuſions; which endeavours to fix upon marble or braſs tranſitory grandeur, that paſſes away with ſo much rapidity; which endeavours to ſecure to itſelf a portion of a worldly life in the very empire of death.

A death bed figure is the moſt humbling ſight in the world: to ſet in ſo dark a cloud, and to go off with languor, convulſions, and deformity, is a terrible rebuke to the pride of human nature.

Worldly glory ends with the world; and, for what concerns us, the world ends with our lives. What have we to be proud of? Are not all things periſhable? The time of flouriſhing pride is ſoon over, and our little greatneſs is loſt in eternity.

Of

Of ENVY and DETRACTION.

A WISE man values himself upon the score of virtue, and not of opinion; and thinks himself neither better nor worse for what others say of him.

Virtue is not secure against envy: men will lessen what they do not imitate.

He that praises, bestows a favour; but he that detracts, commits a robbery.

It is observed, that the most censorious are generally the least judicious; who, having nothing to recommend themselves, will be finding faults with others. No man envies the merit of another, that has any of his own.

Many speak ill, because they never learned to speak well.

He that envies, makes another man's virtue his vice, and another's happiness his torment; whereas he that rejoices at the prosperity of another, is a partaker of the same.

Illnature is a contradiction to the laws of providence, and the interest of mankind;

a punish-

a punifhment, no lefs than a fault, to thofe that have it. *Antoninus*.

The triumph of wit is to make your goodnature fubdue your cenfure; to be quick in feeing faults, and flow in expofing them. *Spec*.

A good word is an eafy obligation; but not to fpeak ill requires only our filence, which cofts us nothing. *Tillotf*.

There is an odious fpirit in many perfons, who are better pleafed to detect a fault, than commend a virtue.

The worthieft people are moft injured by flanderers; as we ufually find that to be the beft fruit, which the birds have been pecking at. *Swift*.

It is a folly for an eminent man to think of efcaping cenfure, and a weaknefs to be affected with it. *Fab. Maximus* faid, he was a greater coward that was afraid of reproach, than he that fled from his enemies.

Socrates, when informed of fome derogating fpeeches one had ufed of him behind his back, made only this facetious reply: let him beat me too, when I am abfent.

A clear confcience fears no accufation.

It

It is harder to avoid cenfure, than to gain applaufe; for this may be done by one great or wife action in an age; but, to efcape cenfure, a man muft pafs his whole life, without faying or doing one ill or foolifh thing.

Envy is fixed only on merit; and, like a fore eye, is offended with every thing that is bright. *Plut.*

A good life does not filence calumny, but it certainly difarms it.

There is feldom any thing uttered in malice, which turns not to the hurt of the fpeaker. Ill reports do harm to him that makes them; and to thofe they are made to, as well as thofe they are made of.

Some have a perfidious trick to ruin a man by commendations; to praife for fmall things, that they may difparage fuccefsfully for greater. It is the worft of malice, fays *Plutarch*, to intermix with reproaches fome praifes, that the accufations may gain the firmer belief.

Philip of Macedon faid, he was beholden to the Athenian orators for reproving him; for he would endeavour both by words and actions to make them liars. And *Plato*, hearing it was afferted by fome perfons that he he was a very bad man, said, I shall take care to live so, that no body will believe them.

Nothing is truly infamous, but what is wicked; and therefore shame can never disturb an innocent and virtuous mind.

The surest sign of a noble disposition is, to have no envy in one's nature.

It is an excellent saying of *Antoninus*, the great emperor and philosopher, no man was ever unhappy for not prying into the actions and conditions of other men; but that man is necessarily unhappy who does not observe himself, and consider the state of his own soul.

Our industrious search and inquiries should chiefly be employed about our own affairs at home; for here we shall find so many offences in our conversation, such variety of perturbations in our souls, and manifest failures in our duty, that it will take up so much time to reform them, as not to leave us any leisure to be impertinent or illnatured in remarking upon the faults of others. *Plut.*

If we well knew how little others enjoy, it would rescue the world from one sin;

there

there would be no such thing as envy upon earth. *Young.*

He that values himself upon conscience, not opinion, never heeds reproaches. When I am ill spoken of, I take it thus: if I have not deserved it, I am never the worse; if I have, I will mend.

The contempt of injurious words stifles them; but resentment revives them.

A man that has no virtue in himself envies it in others. *Bacon.*

In the business of talebearing, a liar has as much credit as any; for slander has more power to persuade, than either reason or eloquence.

Illwill never speaks well, nor does well.

The failings of good men are commonly more published in the world than their good deeds; and one fault of a well-deserving man shall meet with more reproaches, than all his virtues praise: such is the force of illwill and illnature. *Spec.*

Censure is the tax a man pays the public for being eminent.

When any man speaks ill of us, we are to make use of it as a caution, without troubling ourselves at the calumny. He is in a wretched cafe, that values himfelf upon other people's opinions, and depends upon their judgment for the peace of his life.

I do not allow of envy, faid *Euripides,* but fo good I would be envied.

It is in the power of every man to preferve his probity; but no man living has it in his power to fay, that he can preferve his reputation, while there are fo many evil tongues in the world ready to blaft the faireft character; and fo many open ears ready to receive their reports.

Other paffions have objects to flatter them, and feemingly to content and fatisfy them for a while: there is power in ambition, and pleafure in luxury, and pelf in covetoufnefs; but envy can give nothing but vexation. *Montaigne.*

Of

Of HOPE, FEAR, ANXIETY, and DISTRUST.

OUR hopes and fears are the main spring of all our religious endeavours.

There is no condition so low, but may have hopes; nor any so high, that is out of the reach of fears.

It is fancy, not the reason of things, that makes life so uneasy to us as we find it. It is not the place, nor the condition, but the mind alone, that can make any body happy or miserable. *L'Estr.*

Hope makes that present, by a prepossession of that which is to come.

He that wants hope, is the poorest man living.

It is necessary to hope, though hope should always be deluded: for hope itself is happiness, and its frustrations, however frequent, are yet less dreadful than its extinction. *Johnson.*

A wise man, says *Seneca*, is provided for occurrences of any kind; the good he manages, the bad he vanquishes: in prosperity

D   rity

rity he betrays no prefumption, in adverfity he feels no defpondency.

When *Anaxagoras* was told of the death of his fon, he only faid, *I knew he was mortal.* So we, in all cafualties of life, fhould fay, I knew my riches were uncertain, that my friend was but a man. Such confiderations would foon pacify us, becaufe all our troubles proceed from their being unexpected. *Plut.*

Hopes and difappointments, are the lot and entertainment of human life; the one ferves to keep us from prefumption, the other from defpair.

Hope is very fallacious, and promifes what it feldom gives; but its promifes are more valuable than the gifts of fortune, and it feldom fruftrates us without affuring us of recompenfing the delay by great bounty. *Johnfon.*

There is a medium between an exceffive diffidence and too univerfal a confidence. If we have no forefight, we are furprifed; if it is too nice, we are miferable.

The apprehenfion of evil is many times worfe than the evil itfelf; and the ills a man fears he fhall fuffer, he fuffers in the very fear of them.

A noble

A noble spirit must not vary with his fortune: in your worst estate hope; in the best, fear; and, in all, be circumspect.

A man cannot truly be happy here, without a well-grounded hope of being happy hereafter.

A firm trust in the assistance of an almighty Being naturally produces patience, cheerfulness, and all other dispositions of mind that alleviate those calamities which we are not able to remove. *Spec.*

It is virtue only that repels fear, and fear only that makes life troublesome.

If you are disquieted at any thing, you should consider with yourself, is the thing of that worth, that for it I should so disturb myself, and lose my peace and tranquillity? *Antoninus.*

The keeping ourselves above grief, and every painful passion, is indeed very beautiful and excellent; and none but souls of the first rate seem to be qualified for the undertaking. *Char.*

There can be no peace in human life, without the contempt of all events. He that troubles his head with drawing consequences from mere contingencies, shall never be at rest. *L'Estr.*

The

The melancholy perfon always prefages misfortunes.

A poor diftracted man, and a rich diftracted man, are pretty much upon an equality; and, as far as the power of imagination goes, often change conditions; the poor man fancying himfelf a prince, while the rich one pines, and torments himfelf with all the anxieties of poverty.

More perifh through too much confidence than by too much fear: where one defpairs, there are thoufands that prefume.

Fear unbalanced by hope, is defperation.

Doft thou lament for what is to come? Why? becaufe it is not come? No, becaufe it is grievous: and wilt thou double thy griefs, with bringing them on before they come? Why fhould we run forward to meet thofe miferies, which at the fame time we would fain run away from?

Fear is implanted in us as a prefervative from evil; but its duty, like that of other paffions, is not to overbear reafon, but to affift it; nor fhould it be fuffered to tyrannife in the imagination, to raife phantoms of horror, or befet life with fupernumerary diftreffes. *Johnfon.*

The

The thing in the world, fays *Montaigne*, I am moft afraid of, is *fear*; and with good reafon; that paffion alone, in the trouble of it, exceeding all other accidents.

We fhould take a prudent care for the future, but fo as to enjoy the prefent. It is no part of wifdom to be miferable to-day, becaufe we may happen to be fo to-morrow.

Hope is the laft thing that dies in man; and though it be exceeding deceitful, yet it is of this good ufe to us, that while we are travelling through this life, it conducts us an eafier and more pleafant path to our journey's end. *Rochef.*

It were no virtue to bear calamities, if we did not feel them. *Sen.*

Miferies are endlefs, if we ftand in fear of all impoffibilities.

Divine providence always places the remedy near the evil. There is not any duty to which Providence has not annexed a bleffing; nor any affliction for which virtue has not provided a remedy.

If fome are refined, like gold, in the furnace of affliction, there are many more that, like chaff, are confumed in it. Sorrow, when it is exceffive, takes away fervour

D 3 from

from piety, vigour from action, health from the body, light from the reason, and repose from the conscience.

It may serve as a comfort to us in all our calamities and afflictions, that he that loses any thing, and gets wisdom by it, is a gainer by the loss.

When Faith, Temperance, and other celestial powers, left the earth; Hope was the only goddess that staid behind.

The expectation of future happiness is the best relief of anxious thoughts, the most perfect cure of melancholy, the guide of life, and the comfort of death.

Hopes and cares, anger and fears, divide our life. Would you be free from these anxieties; think every day will be your last, and then the succeeding hours will be the more welcome, because unexpected. *Hor.*

There is but one way of fortifying the soul against all gloomy presages and terrors of mind; and that is, by securing to ourselves the friendship and protection of that being, who disposes of events, and governs futurity. *Spec.*

Of the GOVERNMENT of the PASSIONS.

THE utmoft perfection we are capable of in this world, is to govern our lives and actions by the rules which nature has fet us, and keeping the order of our creation. *Spec.*

He is the wife man, who, though not fkilled in fcience, knows how to govern his paffions and affections. Our paffions are our infirmities. He that can make a facrifice of his will, is lord of himfelf.

Paffion has its foundation in nature : virtue is acquired by the improvement of our reafon.

No man is mafter of himfelf, fo long as he is a flave to any thing elfe.

Prudence governs the wife ; but there are only a few of that fort, and the moft wife are not fo at all times ; whereas paffion governs almoft all the world, and at moft times. *St. Evr.*

It is the bafeft of paffions to like what we have not, and flight what we poffefs.

D 4.   Excefs.

Excefs of forrow is as foolifh as profufe laughter. Loud mirth, or immoderate forrow, inequality of behaviour either in profperity or adverfity are alike ungraceful in a man that is born to die. *Spec.*

Paffion is a fort of fever in the mind, which ever leaves us weaker than it found us.

Nothing alleviates grief fo much as the liberty of complaining : nothing makes one more fenfible of joy than the delight of expreffing it.

A man's ftrongeft paffion is generally his weaker fide.

It is certainly much eafier wholly to decline a paffion, than to keep it within juft bounds and meafures ; and that which few can moderate, almoft any body may prevent. *Char.*

Philofophy and religion fhow themfelves in no one inftance fo much as in the preferving our minds firm and fteady.

He that does any thing rafhly, muft be taken, in equity of conftruction, to do it willingly ; for he was free to deliberate or not.

To mourn without meafure is folly ; not to mourn at all, infenfibility.

Abfence

Abfence cools moderate paffions, and inflames violent ones; as the wind blows out candles, but kindles fires. *Rochef.*

Sadnefs contracts the mind; mirth dilates it.

He that refigns his peace to little cafualties, and fuffers the courfe of his life to be interrupted by fortuitous inadvertencies or offences, delivers up himfelf to the direction of the wind, and lofes all that conftancy and equanimity, which conftitute the chief praife of a wife man. *Johnfon.*

The philofopher *Bion* faid pleafantly of the king, who by handfuls pulled his hair off his head for forrow: Does this man think that baldnefs is a remedy for grief?

There is in human nature generally more of the fool, than of the wife; and therefore thofe faculties, by which the foolifh part of mens minds are taken, are more potent. *Bacon.*

Pofitive men err moft of any.

We often hate, we know not why, without examining either the good or bad qualities of the perfon; and this fenfelefs averfion of ours will fometimes fall upon men of extraordinary merit. It is the bufinefs of reafon to correct this blind paffion,

which

which is a reproach to it : for is there any thing more unjuft, than to have an averfion to thofe that are a honour to human nature ?

Paffion makes them fools, which otherwife are not fo; and fhows them to be fools which are fo.

The firft ftep to moderation is, to perceive that we are falling into a paffion. One faying to *Diogenes*, after a fellow had fpit in his face, this affront, fure, will make you angry : *no*, faid he ; *but I am thinking whether I ought not to be fo.*

They that laugh at every thing, and they that fret at every thing, are fools alike.

He that overcomes his paffions, conquers his greateft enemies.

The good government of our appetites, and corrupt inclinations, will make our minds cheerful and eafy : contentment will fweeten a low fortune, and patience will make our fufferings light.

Moderation of paffions, judgment in counfel, and dexterity in affairs, are the moft eminent parts of wifdom.

Plato, fpeaking of paffionate perfons, fays, they are like men who ftand on their heads, they fee all things the wrong way.

To

To be mafters of ourfelves and habits, it is indifpenfably neceffary, that our thoughts be good and regular, which is effected by good converfe either with books or perfons: hence we may know ourfelves, and adapt particular remedies to our weakneffes; for there is nothing impoffible that is neceffary to the accomplifhment of our happinefs.

No man, whofe appetites are his mafters, can perform the duties of his nature with ftrictnefs and regularity. He that would be fuperior to external influences, muft firft become fuperior to his own paffions. *Johnfon.*

Sobriety and temperance of all kinds, moderate exercife, appetites well governed, and keeping one's felf from melancholy, and all violent paffion and diforder of the mind, do affift, preferve, confirm, and finifh, what nature and complexion at firft began. *Char.*

Of VANITY, FOLLY, and AFFECTATION.

TO be covetous of applause difcovers a flender merit; and felf-conceit is the ordinary attendant of ignorance. *Spec.*

The moft ignorant are moft conceited, and the moft impatient of advice, as unable to difcern either their own folly, or the wifdom of others.

Young men, when they are once died in pleafure and vanity, will fcarcely take any other colour.

There are a thoufand fops made by art, for one fool by nature.

It is to affectation the world owes its whole race of coxcombs: nature in her whole drama never drew fuch a part; fhe has fometimes made a fool, but a coxcomb is always of a man's own making.

Some would be thought to do great things, who are but tools or inftruments: like the fool that fancied he played upon the organ, when he only drew the bellows.

They

They are more dangeroufly ill, that are drunk with vanity, than thofe with wine; for a morning makes one himfelf, but the other is unrecoverable.

Oftentation takes from the merit of any action. He that is vain enough to cry up himfelf, ought to be punifhed with the filence of other men.

The obfervation that no man is ridiculous for being what he is, but only in the affectation of being fomething more, is equally true in regard to the mind and the body. *Guard.*

Men are as apt to defend their opinions, as their property; and would take it as well to have the titles to their eftates queftioned, as their fenfe.

Socrates had fo little efteem of himfelf, that he thought he knew nothing certainly, *but that he knew nothing.*

It is a common obfervation, that no man is content with his own condition, though it be the beft; nor diffatisfied with his own wit, though it be the worft.

Every man has as much vanity, as he wants underftanding. An afs was carrying an image in proceffion; and, feeing the people fall down every where upon their knees before him, the filly animal fancied all this while that they worfhipped him.

Some men affect the oftentation of bufinefs, feeming always to be fully employed, though without materially doing any thing: fuch are rather bufy men, than men of bufinefs.

The vanity of human life is like a river conftantly paffing away, and yet conftantly coming on.   *Swift.*

It is the infirmity of poor fpirits to be taken with every appearance, and dazzled with every thing that fparkles: but great geniufes have but little admiration, becaufe few things appear new to them.

Though a coat be ever fo fine that a fool wears, it is ftill but a fool's coat.   *Spec.*

The monftrous affectation of our travelled gentlemen and ladies to fpeak in the French air, to drefs, to cook, to write in French, has corrupted at once our language and our manners.   *Felton.*

The ftrongeft paffions allow us fome reft; but vanity keeps us perpetually in motion. What a duft do I raife! fays the fly upon the coach-wheel: and what a rate do I drive at! fays the fame fly upon the horfe's buttock.

Opinionative

Opinionative men will believe nothing but what they can comprehend; and there are but few things that they are able to comprehend. *St. Evr.*

It was a wife saying of *Ariftotle* to an indiscreet and conceited person, that he wished he was what the other thought himself to be; and that his enemies were such as he was.

A seeming modesty, is a surer evidence of vanity, than a moderate degree of assurance. A gnat that had planted himself upon the horn of a bull, very civilly begged the bull's pardon: but rather than incommode you, says he, I will remove.

When men will not be reasoned out of a vanity, they must be ridiculed out of it. *L'Eftr.*

Some put so much weight upon show and ornaments, that even the thought of death is made less heavy to them by the contemplation of their being laid out in state, and honorably attended to the grave. *Halifax.*

A wife man endeavours to shine in himself, a fool to outshine others: the first is humbled by the sense of his own infirmities; the last lifted up by the discovery of those which
which

which he obferves in others. The wife man confiders what he wants, and the fool what he abounds in. The wife man is happy, when he gains his own approbation; and the fool, when he recommends himfelf to the applaufe of thofe about him.

Of all forts of affectation, that which is moft incurable, is the affectation of wifdom; becaufe the difeafe is in the remedy itfelf, and falls upon reafon, which only could and ought to cure it, if it were any-where elfe.

Of HUMAN LEARNING; ITS USE AND INSUFFICIENCY.

MAN thinks it the finest thing in the world to know much; and therefore is greatly apt to esteem himself better than his neighbours, if he knows some little impertinences, and them imperfectly, with infinite uncertainty. *Taylor.*

We live in an age, when men are fond of learning, almost to the loss of religion. Nothing will pass with our men of wit and sense, but what is agreeable with the nicest reason; and every man's reason is his own understanding. These mighty pretenders have no truer ground to go upon, than other men: they plead for right reason; but they mean their own. In the mean time they take from us our surest guide, and religion suffers by their contentions about it. *Baker.*

Philosophy is then only valuable, when it serves for the law of life, and not the ostentation of science.

Though a man may not be a logician or naturalist, yet he is never the further off

by

by it from being either liberal, or modeft, or charitable. *Antoninus.*

No knowledge which terminates in curiofity and fpeculation, is comparable to that which is of ufe: and of all ufeful knowledge, that is moft fo, which confifts in a due care, and juft notion of ourfelves. *St. Bernard.*

Rectitude of will is a greater ornament and perfection, than brightnefs of underftanding; and to be divinely good, more valuable than any other wifdom and knowledge.

However we may be puffed up with vain conceits of new worlds of learning; it is certain we are yet much in the dark; that many of our difcoveries are purely imaginary; and that the ftates of learning is fo far from perfection, much more from being the fubject of oftentation, that it ought to teach us modefty, and keep us humble. *Baker.*

Some are fo very ftudious of learning what was done by the ancients, that they know not how to live with the moderns.

Every man who propofes to grow eminent by learning, fhould carry in his mind

at

at once the difficulty of excellence, and the force of induſtry; and remember that fame is not conferred but as the recompence of labour; and that labour, vigorouſly continued, has not often failed of its reward. *Johnſon.*

A man of ſenſe does not ſo much apply himſelf to the moſt learned writings, in order to acquire knowledge; as the moſt rational, to fortify his reaſon. *St. Evr.*

Ariſtippus ſaid, that the only fruit he had received from his philoſophy, was to ſpeak plainly to all the world, and to tell freely his thoughts of things.

To preſerve the intire liberty of one's judgment, without being prepoſſeſſed with falſe reaſons, or pretended authority, is a ſtrength of mind whereof few are capable.

The ſuperfine ſubtilties of the ſchools ſpeak many ſharp things, but utterly unneceſſary, and void of effect. Too much refining deſtroys pure reaſon. *Spec.*

Fine ſenſe and exalted ſenſe, are not half ſo uſeful as common ſenſe. *Swift.*

Men are apt to overvalue the tongues, and to think they have made a conſiderable progreſs in learning when they have once overcome theſe; yet in reality there is no
internal

internal worth in them, and men may understand a thousand languages without being the wiser.   *Baker.*

A sincere confession of our ignorance, is one of the fairest and surest testimonies of our judgment.   *Montaigne.*

What is the whole creation, but one great library: every volume in which, and every page in these volumes, are impressed with radiant characters of infinite wisdom; and all the perfections of the universe are contracted with such inimitable art in man, that he needs no other book but himself to make him a complete philosopher.

There is no end of books. Our libraries are furnished for sight and ostentation rather than use; the very indexes are not to be read over in an age; and in this multitude, how great a part of them are either dangerous, or not worth the reading! A few books, well chosen, and well made use of, will be more profitable, than a great confused library.

One would admire how it is possible for a wise man to spend his life in unprofitable inquiries. Some men, says *St Evremond,* make a merit of knowing what they might as well be ignorant of, and are absolute strangers to what is really worth knowing.

Lycurgus

Lycurgus remarked, that fubtile fpecula-tions, and all the refinements of fcience, ferved to fpoil the underftanding, and cor-rupt the heart; for which reafon he made little account of them.

Moft men take leaft notice of what is plain, as if that were of no ufe; but puzzle their thoughts, and lofe themfelves in thofe vaft depths and abyffes, which no human underftanding can fathom. *Sherlock.*

The ways of nature, like thofe of GOD, are paft man's finding out. *Baker.*

To be proud of learning is the greateft ignorance. *Taylor.*

It is a filly conceit, that men without languages are alfo without underftand-ing: it is apparent in all ages, that fome fuch have been even prodigies for ability; for it is not to be believed, that wifdom fpeaks to her difciples only in Latin, Greek, and Hebrew. *Fuller.*

Marius did never blufh to profefs before the fenate his being ignorant of Greek, and his careleffnefs in being otherwife; con-fidering how little he obferved it helped fuch as were fkilled therein to the purch-afing of virtue.

The

. The pains we take in books or arts, which treat of things remote from the use of life, is a busy idleness.

There is no necessity of being led through the several fields of knowledge : it will be sufficient to gather some of the fairest fruit from them all; and to lay up a store of good sense, sound reason, and solid virtue. *Felton.*

It is the work of fancy to enlarge, but of judgment to shorten and contract ; and therefore this must needs be as far above the other, as judgment is a greater and nobler faculty, than fancy or imagination.

The variety of opinions among the learned manifests, that there can be no certainty, where there is so much dissent.

We rarely meet with persons that have a true judgment; which, in many, renders literature a very tiresome knowledge. Good judges are as rare as good authors. *St. Evr.*

It happens to men truly learned, as to ears of corn; they shoot up and raise their heads high, while they are empty ; but when full and swelled with grain, they begin to flag and droop. *Montaigne.*

We read of a philosopher, who declared of himself, that the first year he entered

upon

upon the ftudy of philofophy, he knew all things; the fecond year he knew fomething; but the third year nothing: the more he ftudied, the more he declined in the opinion of his own knowledge, and faw more of the fhortnefs of his underftanding.

The curiofity of feeing into every thing, explaining every thing, and adjufting it to our weak ideas, is the moft dangerous difeafe of the human mind.

That good fenfe, fays *Comines*, which nature affords us, is preferable to moft of the knowledge that we can acquire.

Of all parts of wifdom, the practice is the beft. *Socrates* was efteemed the wifeft man of his time, becaufe he turned his acquired knowledge into morality, and aimed at goodnefs more than greatnefs.

A curfory knowledge, though it be not exact enough for the fhoots, is more pleafant, and perhaps more ufeful, than to overburden the brain with reading intricate and voluminous authors.

Men gain little by philofophy, but the means to fpeak probably of every thing, and to make themfelves be admired by the lefs knowing. *Defcartes*.

He

He who wants good fenfe, is unhappy in having learning; for he has thereby only more ways of expofing himfelf. *Tat.*

Subtile fophiftry perverts true philofophy.

Wrangling about frivolous criticifms in words, though it is a great part of the bufinefs of a fchool, is too pedantic and low for a generous converfe; while he that is well grown in knowledge may perhaps forget, or not fo much refpect, the firft rudiments of letters; it being more grateful to the mind to contemplate the ftructures of learning, as they ftand finifhed and adorned, than to difcufs the low materials of their foundations.

One philofopher is worth a thoufand grammarians. Good fenfe and reafon ought to be the umpire of all rules, both ancient and modern. *Rochef.*

True eloquence is good fenfe, delivered in a natural and unaffected way, without the artificial ornaments of tropes and figures. Our common eloquence is ufually a cheat upon the underftanding; it deceives us with appearances inftead of things, and makes us think we fee reafon, while it is only tickling our fenfe. *Baker.*

Obfcurity

Obfcurity in writing is commonly an argument of darkneſs in the mind: the greateſt learning is to be ſeen in the greateſt plainneſs. *Wilkins.*

It is an idle fancy of ſome to run out perpetually upon ſimilitudes, confounding their ſubject by the multitude of likeneſſes, and making it like nothing at all.

Difficult and abſtruſe ſpeculations raiſe a noiſe and a duſt; but, when we examine what account they turn to, little comes of them, but heat, and clamour, and contradiction. *Charron.*

The reaſon of things lies in a narrow compaſs, if the mind could at any time be ſo happy as to light it up. Moſt of the writings and diſcourſes in the world are but illuſtration and rhetoric; which ſignifies as much as nothing to a mind in purſuit after the philoſophical truth of things. *South.*

Though it may be an argument of a great wit to give ingenious reaſons for many wonderful appearances in nature; yet it is an evidence of ſmall judgment, to be poſitive in any thing but the knowledge of our own ignorance.

E   It

It paſſes for an ornament to borrow from other tongues, where we may be better furniſhed in our own. *Spec.*

Pedantry is a vice in all profeſſions, itſelf no profeſſion.

Suppoſe a man knows what is Greek, Latin, French, Spaniſh, or Italian for a *horſe*; this makes the man no more the wiſer, than the horſe the better. *Blunt.*

Languages are not to be deſpiſed; but things are to be ſtill preferred.

One of the ancients, who was reproached that he profeſſed philoſophy, for which he nevertheleſs in his own judgment made no great account; made anſwer, *that this was truly to philoſphize.*

The moſt reſplendent ornament of man is judgment; here is the perfection of his innate reaſon; here is the utmoſt power of reaſon joined with knowledge.

It is no ſmall progreſs in philoſophy to have learned how much obſcurity and uncertainty is mingled with our exacteſt knowledge, and to be ſatisfied to be ignorant of that which cannot be known.

There are impertinent ſtudies, as well as impertinent men. *Seneca.*

I:

It was a faying of *Cicero*, that oratory was but his ornament, as a commonwealth man; and that philofophy and reafon were his profeffion, as a man.

Phocion was preferred before *Demoſthenes*, in that he always filled his fpeeches with fubſtantial matter. He was fparing of rhetoric, and full of reafon.

Such books as teach fapience and prudence, and ferve to eradicate errors and vices, are the moſt profitable writings in the world, and ought to be valued and ſtudied more than all others whatſoever.

Inſtead of labouring in nice learning, and intricate fciences; inſtead of trifling away precious time upon the fecrets of nature, or myſteries of ſtate; it were better to feek that only which is really and ſubſtantially good. Our pains ſhould be to moderate our hopes and fears; to direct and regulate our paſfions; to bear all injuries of fortune or men, and to attain the art of contentment; and then we cannot have much more to wiſh for.

Art is long, and life but ſhort. *Hipp.*

The wiſdom of the ancients, as to the government of life, was no more than certain precepts what to do, and what not; and

E 2 men

men were much better in that fimplicity; for, as they came to be more learned, they grew lefs careful of being good. That plain and open virtue is now turned into a dark and intricate fcience; and we are taught to difpute, rather than to live. *Seneca.*

If I ftudy, fays *Montaigne,* it is for no other fcience, than what treats of the knowledge of myfelf, and inftructs me how to live and die well.

The *Lacedæmonians* applied their minds to no learning but what was ufeful; and would not fuffer the profeffors of any fpeculative fciences to live in their government, left by their difputations, and empty notions, they fhould deprave the true excellency of virtue. *Plut.*

It is a miftake to think, that a large fyftem of ethics, diffected according to the nice prefcriptions of logic, and methodically replenifhed with definitions, divifions, diftinctions, and fyllogifms, is requifite or fufficient to make men virtuous. The actual poffeffion of one virtue is preferable to the bare fpeculative knowledge of all arts and fciences together. *Boyle.*

The moral hilofophy of *Ariftotle,* Socrates, *Plato,* &c. can make men only philofophers,

phers, and are too weak to make them thoroughly good; neither is it any of their fair maxims, that patience in affliction, and fortitude against adversity, are to be found.

There are a great many speculations, which divines trouble themselves and the world with, which, they themselves do yet confess, are not necessary to any man's salvation; and consequently, which a man is no more obliged to busy his head with, than with any problems in geometry. *Synge.*

Our controversies about religion have brought at last even religion itself into controversy. The schoolmen have spun the thread too fine, and made christianity look more like a course of philosophy, than a system of faith, and supernatural revelation: so that the spirit of it evaporates into niceties, and exercises of the brain; and the contention is not for truth but victory. *L'Estr.*

A good man will see his duty with only a moderate share of casuistical skill; but into a perverse heart this sort of wisdom enters not. Were men as much afraid of sin, as they are of danger, there would be few occasions of consulting our casuists. *Baker.*

F. 3   Men

Men that are deftitute of religion, fays *Lactantius*, are fo far from being learned philofophers, that they ought not to be efteemed fo much as reafonable men.

Knowledge will not be acquired without pains and application. It is troublefome and deep digging for pure waters; but when once you come to the fpring, they rife up, and meet you. *Felton.*

Learning is preferable to riches, and virtue to both.

There is nothing good, or evil, but virtue, or vice. What is knowledge good for which does not direct and govern our lives? *Sherlock.*

Ufeful knowledge can have no enemies, except the ignorant: it cherifhes youth, delights the aged, is an ornament in profperity, and yields comfort in adverfity.

Knowledge, that is of ufe, muft be allowed to be the greateft and the nobleft acquift that man can gain. But to run on in their difputations, whether privation be a principle; whether any thing can be made of nothing; whether there be an empty fpace in the compaf of nature; or whether the world fhould have an end, and fuchlike; is without end, and to no end.

The

The diffusion of the mind into variety of thoughts and subjects, renders it incapable of any deep search.

Wise men are instructed by reason; men of less understanding, by experience; the most ignorant, by necessity; and beasts by nature. *Cicero.*

It is an argument of a truly brave disposition in a learned man, not to assume the name and character of one. *Plut.*

Though the simplest man knows he has the faculties of imagination, apprehension, memory, reflection; yet the most learned cannot assign where they are seated, or by what means they operate.

The two most essential points in moral philosophy are a last end, and the means to attain it; and that beatitude consists in the noblest action of man in reference to the most excellent object. *A. iffot.*

If our painful peregrination in studies be destitute of the supreme light, it is nothing else but a miserable kind of wandering. *Scaliger.*

It is with the mind as with the will and appetites: for as, after we have tried a thousand pleasures, and turned from one enjoyment to another, we find no rest to

our defires, till we at laft fix them upon the
fovereign good; fo, in purfuit of knowledge, we meet with no tolerable fatisfaction to our minds, till, after we are wearied
with tracing other methods, we turn them
at laft upon the one fupreme and unerring
truth. And where there no other ufe of
human learning, there is at leaft this in it,
that by its many defects it brings us to a
fenfe of our own weaknefs, and makes us
more readily, and with greater willingnefs,
fubmit to revelation. *Baker*.

True philofophy, fays *Plato*, confifts
more in fidelity, conftancy, juftice, fincerity,
and in the love of our duty, than in great
capacity.

The balm which philofophy drops upon
the wounds of the mind, abates their pain,
though it cannot heal them. *Johnfon*.

The main opportunity for knowledge is
after this life; but the only opportunity of
being good is *now*; and, if we take care to
improve this, we are fufficiently fecure of
the other; but if this be neglected, all is
loft.

We know little of the caufes of things,
but may fee wifdom enough in every thing:
and could we be content to fpend as much
time

time in contemplating the wife ends of providence, as we do in fearching into caufes,
it would certainly make us better men, and
not worfe philofophers. *Baker.*

It was a ufeful faying of *Pafcal,* that
fciences produced no confolation in the
times of afflidtion; but the knowledge of
chriftianity was a comfort both in adverfity,
and defed of all other knowledge.

The height of all philofophy, both natural and moral, is to *know thyfelf*; and the
end of this knowledge is to know GOD.

In vain do we feek for a true and lafting
fatisfadtion, in any other books than the holy
fcriptures; wherein are contained all things
neceffary to the happinefs of this and the
life hereafter.

As the moon, for all thofe darker parts
we call fpots, gives us a much greater light
than the ftars, that feem all luminous, fo
do the fcriptures afford more light than the
brighteft human authors: in them the ignorant may learn all requifite knowledge, and
the moft knowing may learn to difcern their
ignorance. *Boyle.*

There is but one way to heaven for the
learned and unlearned. *Taylor.*

E 5 IIc

He that knows what belongs to his salvation, has learned what is sufficient. *Bona.*

At the day of judgment, thou shalt not be asked, what proficiency thou hast made in logic, metaphysics, astronomy, or any other science; but whether thou hast lived according to thy nature, as a man endued with reason and morality. *Turk. Spy.*

Were matters so managed, that men turned their speculation into practice, and took care to apply their reading to the purposes of human life; the advantage of learning would be unspeakable; and we see how illustriously such persons shine in the world: and therefore nothing can be said to the prejudice of learning in general, but only to such a false opinion of it, as depends upon this alone for the most eligible, and only qualification of the mind of man; and so rests upon it, and buries it in inactivity. *Charron.*

All things else being transitory and perishing, the true wisdom is to think of eternity; and to be a good man is the best of philosophies.

Of PROSPERITY and ADVERSITY; CONTENTMENT and HUMILITY.

IT may boldly be affirmed, that good men generally reap more fubftantial benefit from their afflictions, than bad men do from their profperities; and what they lofe in wealth, pleafure, or honour, they gain with vaft advantage in wifdom and goodnefs, and tranquillity of mind. *Scott.*

Contentment excludes all murmuring and repining at the allotments of Providence; all folicitude and anxious thoughts about future events, farther than fuch precautions as are within the fphere of human prudence.

The compendious addrefs to wealth, as *Pluto* obferved, is not to increafe poffeffions, but leffen defires.

Profperity is not without its troubles, nor adverfity without its comforts.

A good man, whether he be rich or poor, fhall at all times rejoice with a cheerful countenance.

There is fcarce any lot fo low, but there is fomething in it to fatisfy the man whom

it

it has befallen; Providence having fo ordered things, that in every man's cup, how bitter foever, there are fome cordial drops, which, if wifely extracted, are fufficient to make him contented. *Sterne.*

Contentment is only to be found within ourfelves. A man that is content with a little, has enough; he that complains, has too much.

If you can live free from want, care for no more; for the reft is but vanity. *Raleigh.*

He that can well endure, may, without difficulty, overcome.

The confideration of a greater evil is a fort of remedy againft a leffer. *Ariftippus* had a farm burnt down; and, when a friend of his expreffed a concern for him, he said, I have three farms yet left, and thou haft but one in all; and have more reafon to lament thy misfortune, than thou mine. *Plut.*

To live, nature affordeth; to live content, wifdom teacheth.

A very little is fufficient for a man well nurtured.

If we will create imaginary wants to ourfelves, why do we not create imaginary
fatis-

satisfaction to them? It were the merrier phrenſy of the two to be like the *Athenian*, who fancied all the ſhips that came into the harbour, were his own.

Socrates rightly ſaid of contentment, oppoſing it to the riches of fortune and opinion, that it is the wealth of nature; for it gives every thing that we want, and really need.

Proſperity has always been the cauſe of far greater evils to men, than adverſity: and it is eaſier for a man to bear this patiently, than not to forget himſelf in the other.

Moderation in proſperity, is a virtue very difficult to all mortals. *Johnſon.*

They are always impaired by affliction, who are not thereby improved.

Among all other virtues, *humility*, though it be loweſt, yet is preeminent: it is the ſafeſt, becauſe it is always at anchor; and that man may be truly ſaid to live with moſt content in his calling, that ſtrives to live within the compaſs of it. *Richl.*

Proud men never have friends; neither in proſperity, becauſe they know nobody; nor in adverſity, becauſe then nobody knows them.

He

He who thinks no man above him but for his virtue, none below him but for his vice, can never be obfequious or affuming in a wrong place. *Tat.*

That which is a neceffity to him that ftruggles, is little other than choice to him that is willing. It is better to be forced to any thing; but things are eafy when they are complied with. *Sen.*

Many afflictions may befäl a good man, but no evil; for contraries will never incorporate. All the rivers in the world are never able to change the tafte and quality of the fea.

Adverfity does not take from us our true friends; it only difperfes thofe who pretended to be fuch.

Wealth and titles are only the gifts of fortune; but peace and content are the peculiar endowments of a well difpofed mind; a mind that can bear affliction without a murmur, and the weight of a plentiful fortune without vain glory; that can be familiar without meannefs, and referved without pride.

We muft needs have fome concern when we look into our loffes: but, if we confider how

how little we deferve what is left, our mur-murs will turn into thankfulnefs.

If thou faint in the day of adverfity, thy ftrength is fmall.

The difcontents of the poor are much eafier allayed than thofe of the rich.

I find it a very hard thing, fays *Montaigne*, to undergo misfortunes; but to be content with a competent meafure of fortune, and to avoid greatnefs, I think a very eafy mat-ter.

Solon being afked by *Cræfus*, who, in the whole world was happier than he; anfwer-ed, *Tellus*, who though he was poor, was a good man, and content with what he had, and died in good old age.

Nothing could be more unhappy, faid *Demetrius*, than a man who had never known affliction.

The beft need afflictions for trial of their virtue : how can we exercife the grace of contentment, if all things fucceed well ? Or that of forgivenefs, if we have no enemies ?

A good confcience is to the foul what health is to the body; it preferves a con-ftant eafe and ferenity within us, and more
than

than countervails all the calamities and af-flictions which can poffibly befal us. *Addif.*

The greateft misfortune of all is not to be able to bear misfortune. *Bias.*

If we would begin at the right end, and look with as much compaffion on the ad-verfities of fome, as we do with envy at the profperities of others, every man would find caufe to fit down contentedly with his own burden.

He that needs leaft, faid *Socrates*, is moft like the gods, who need nothing.

When *Alexander* faw *Diogenes* fitting in the warm fun, and afked what he fhould do for him? He defired no more, than that he would ftand out of his funfhine, and not take from him what he could not give.

A man cannot be unhappy under the moft depreffed circumftances, if he ufes his reafon, not his opinion : and the moft ex-alted fortunes are (if reafon be not confulted) the fubject of a wife man's pity.

The moft excellent of moral virtues is to have a low efteem of ourfelves; which has this particular advantage, that it attracts not the envy of others.

A quiet

A quiet and contented mind is the fupreme good, the utmoſt felicity man is capable of in this world; and the maintaining ſuch an uninterrupted tranquillity of ſpirit is the very crown and glory of wiſdom.

The foundation of content muſt ſpring up in a man's own mind; and he who has ſo little knowledge of human nature as to ſeek happineſs by changing any thing but his own diſpoſition, will waſte his life in fruitleſs efforts, and multiply the griefs which he purpoſes to remove.   *Johnſon.*

Contentment is of that price that it cannot be had at too great a purchaſe, ſince without it the beſt condition in life cannot make us happy, and with it, it is impoſſible we ſhould be miſerable even in the worſt. *Sterne.*

This is the foundation of contentment in all conditions, and of patience under ſufferings; that death, which is not far off, when it removes us out of this world, will take us from all the ſufferings of it. *Sherlock.*

Of FRIENDSHIP.

WE should choose a friend endued with virtue, as a thing in itself lovely and desirable; which consists in a sweet and obliging temper of mind, and a lively readiness in doing good offices. *Plut.*

It was ever my opinion, says *Horace*, that a cheerful goodnatured friend, is so great a blessing, that it admits of no comparison but itself.

Cicero used to say, that it was no less an evil for man to be without a friend, than to have the heavens without a sun. And *Socrates* thought friendship the sweetest possession, and that no piece of ground yielded more or pleasanter fruit, than a true friend.

True friends are the whole world to one another; and he that has a friend to himself is also a friend to mankind. There is no relish in the possession of any thing, without a partner. *Sen.*

It is no flattery to give a friend a due character; for commendation is as much the duty of a friend, as reprehension. *Plut.*

Only

Only good and wife men can be friends; others are but companions.

It is a strange thing to behold what gross errors and extreme absurdities, many (especially of the greater sort) do commit, for want of a friend to tell them of them, to the great damage both of their fame and fortune. *Bacon.*

More hearts pine away in secret anguish, for unkindness from those who should be their comforters, than for any other calamity in life. *Young.*

Worthy minds deny themselves many advantages, to satisfy a generous benevolence, which they bear to their friends in distress. *Spec.*

The kindnesses of a friend lie deep; and whether present, or absent, as occasion serves, he is solicitous about our concerns. *Plut.*

A friendship with a generous stranger is commonly more steady than with the nearest relation.

If the minds be consonant, the best friendship is between different fortunes.

The greater a man is, the more need he has of a friend, and the more difficulty there is of finding and knowing him.

Liberality

Liberality is the beft way to gain affection; for we are affured of their friendfhip, to whom we are obliged. *St. Evr.*

A forwardnefs to oblige is a great grace upon a kindnefs, and doubles the intrinfic worth. In thefe cafes, that which is done with pleafure, is always received fo.

There is no preeminence among true friends; for whether they are equally accomplifhed, or not, they are equally affected to one another. *Plut.*

Anger among friends is unnatural; and therefore, when it happens, is more tormenting. *Young.*

He will find himfelf in a great miftake, that either feeks for a friend in a palace, or tries him at a feaft. *Sen.*

True friendfhip is made up of virtue, as a thing lovely; of familiar converfation, as pleafant; and advantage, as neceffary.

Nothing can impair perfect friendfhip; becaufe truth is the only bond of it.

Friendfhip improves happinefs and abates mifery, by the doubling of our joy, and dividing of our grief. *Cicero.*

An eftranged friend is apt to overflow with tendernefs and remorfe, when a perfon

that

that was once efteemed by him undergoes any misfortune. *Spec.*

To part with a tried friend without very great provocation, is unreafonable levity: nothing but plain malevolence can juftify difunion; malevolence fhewn either in a fingle outrage unretracted, or in habitual illnature. *Col.*

That friendfhip may be at once fond and lafting, there muft not only be equal virtue on each part, but virtue of the fame kind; not only the fame end muft be propofed, but the fame means muft be approved by both. *Johnfon.*

A gentle acceptance of courtefies is as material to maintain friendfhip, as bountitiful prefents.

Many begin friendfhip, and cancel them on flight occafions; and great enmity often fucceeds to a tender affection.

If you have not the indulgence to pardon your friends, nor they the fame to pardon you, your friendfhip will laft no longer than it can ferve both your interefts.

The beft friendfhip is to prevent a requeft, and never put a man to the confufion of afking. To *afk* is a word that lies heavily on the tongue, and cannot well be
uttered

uttered but with a dejected countenance. We should therefore strive to meet our friend in his wishes, if we cannot prevent him.

A man may have a thousand intimate acquaintance, and not a friend among them all. If you have one friend, think yourself happy.

It is a certain principle, that friendship cannot long subsist between many persons. *St. Evr.*

Prosperity is no just scale. Adversity is the only balance to weigh friends. *Plut.*

A great advantage of friendship is the opportunity of receiving good advice: it is dangerous relying always upon our own opinion. Miserable is his case, who, when he needs, has none to admonish him.

When once you profess yourself a friend, endeavour to be always such: he can never have any true friends, that will be often changing them.

Though we ought not to love our friends only for the good they do us; yet it is plain they love not us, if they do not assist us when it is in their power.

To

To owe an obligation to a worthy friend is a happiness, and can be no disparagement. *Charron.*

Gratitude preserves old friendship, and procures new.

Being sometimes asunder heightens friendship. The great cause of the frequent quarrels between relations is their being so much together.

An enemy that disguises himself under the veil of friendship, is worse than he who declares open hostility.

False is their conceit, who say, the way to have a friend is, not to make use of him. Nothing can have greater assurance, that two men are friends, than when experience makes them mutually acknowledge it.

As he that has but a few books, and those good, may receive more improvement from them, than another who has a great number of indifferent ones; so it is in the choice of our friends; no matter how few, so they be discreet and virtuous.

Wealth without friends is like life without health: the one an uncomfortable fortune; the other a miserable being.

Friendship

Friendſhip can never ſuffer ſo much by any other kind of wrong, as by that of a cauſeleſs ſuſpicion.

Nothing is more grievous than the loſs of his friendſhip, whom we have greatly eſteemed, and leaſt feared would fail us. *Spec.*

A friendſhip of intereſts laſts no longer than the intereſt continues; whereas true affection is of the nature of a diamond, it is laſting, and it is hard to break.

Without friends the world is but a wilderneſs. *Bacon.*

A man may eaſily ſecure himſelf from open and profeſſed enemies; but, from ſuch as under a pretence of amity deſign him injury, there is no ſanctuary. Who would imagine that a pleaſing countenance could harbour villainy; or that a ſmile could ſit upon the face of miſchief?

Whoſoever would reclaim his friend, and bring him to a true and perfect underſtanding of himſelf, may privately admoniſh, never publicly reprehend him. An open admonition is an open diſgrace.

As certain rivers are never ſo uſeful as when they overflow; ſo has friendſhip nothing more excellent in it than exceſs; and

doth

doth rather offend in her moderation, than in her violence.

A faithful friend is the medicine of life, and his excellency is invaluable.

Friendſhip has a noble effeċt upon all accidents and conditions: it relieves our cares, raiſes our hopes and abates our fears. A friend, who relates his ſucceſs, talks himſelf into a new pleaſure: and, by opening his misfortunes, leaves part of them behind him.

Proſperity gains friends, and adverſity tries them.

All men have their frailties. Whoever looks for a friend without imperfeċtions, will never find what he ſeeks: we love ourſelves with all our faults, and we ought to love our friend in like manner.

Charity is friendſhip in *common*, and friendſhip is charity *inclojed.*

It is with ſincere affeċtion or friendſhip, as with ghoſts and apparitions; a thing that every body talks of, and ſcarce any has ſeen. *Rochef.*

Friends muſt be preſerved with good deeds, and enemies reconciled with fair words.

F   Whoever

Whoever moves you to part with a true and tried friend, has certainly a defign to make way for a treacherous enemy.

He is happy, that finds a true friend in extremity: but he much more fo, who finds not extremity whereby to try his friend. *Ariftotle.*

No man can lay himfelf under an obligation to do an ill thing. *Pericles*, when one of his friends importuned his fervice in an unjuft matter, excufed himfelf, faying, *I am a friend as far as the altar.*

It was a good fpeech of *Diogenes*, we have need of faithful friends, or fevere enemies.

Friendfhip is the moft facred of all moral bonds. Trufts of confidence, though without any exprefs ftipulation or caution, are yet, in the very nature of them, as facred as if they were guarded with a thoufand articles or conditions. *L'Eftr.*

A true and faithful friend is a living treafure; a comfort in folitude, and a fanctuary in diftrefs.

Some cafes are fo nice, that a man cannot appear in them himfelf, but muft leave the foliciting wholly to his friend. For the purpofe: a man cannot recommend himfelf

without

without vanity, nor afk many times without uneafinefs : but a kind proxy will do juftice to his merits, and relieve his modefty and effect his bufinefs without trouble or blufhing. *Col.*

A friend cannot be known in profperity, and an enemy cannot be hidden in adverfity.

That friendfhip which confifts only in the reciprocation of civil offices, is but a kind of traffic ; and it abides no longer than while fuch men can be ufeful to one another. It is a negociation, not a friendfhip, that has an eye to advantages.

An enemy may receive hurt by our hatred ; but a friend will fuffer a greater injury by our diffimulation. *St. Evr.*

Some enemies, as well as friends, are neceffary ; they make us more circumfpect, more diligent, wifer, and better.

One friend is not bound to bear a part in the follies of another, but rather to diffuade him from them ; and, if he cannot prevail, to tell him plainly, as *Phocion* did *Antipater*, I cannot be both your friend and flatterer. *Plut.*

Hearts may agree, though heads differ.

F 2

Mifery,

Mifery, without a friend to bear a part, is very afflicting; and happinefs, without communication, is tedious; and, as *Seneca* has obferved, fometimes inclines us to make a voluntary choice of mifery for novelty.

There is requifite to friendfhip more goodnefs and virtue, than dexterity of wit, or height of underftanding; it being enough that men have fufficient prudence to be as good as they fhould be, in order to the completing a virtuous friendfhip.

It is better to be judge, faid *Bias*, between ftrangers, than between intimates; for by the firft, one is fure to gain a friend, and by the other an enemy.

It is difficult to act the part of a true friend; for many times, by telling him of his failings, we lofe his affection; and, if we are filent we betray our own confidence. But we cannot lofe a friend in a more honorable way, than in feeking by goodnefs to preferve him.

It will be very fit for all that have entered into any ftrict friendfhip, to make this one fpecial article in the agreement, that they fhall mutally admonifh and reprove each other.

Whatever

Whatever is excellent, has moſt of unity: and as a river, divided into ſeveral ſtreams, is more weak; ſo friendſhip, ſhared among many, is always languid and impotent.

As it is virtue which ſhould determine us in the choice of our friends; ſo it is that alone which we ſhould always regard in them; without inquiring into their good or ill fortune. *Bruyere.*

If a man be entertaining in his diſcourſe, and obliging in his actions; all that friend-ſhip pretends to, is done effectually. *Char.*

A true friend unboſoms freely, adviſes juſtly, aſſiſts readily, adventures boldly, takes all patiently, defends courageouſly, and continues a friend unchangeable.

Of

Of COMPANY, CONVERSATION, and DEPORTMENT.

NOTHING more engages the affections of men, than a handsome address, and graceful conversation. *Spec.*

It is to the virtue and errors of our conversation and ordinary deportment, that we owe both our enemies and our friends, our good or bad character abroad, our domestic peace and troubles, and, in a high degree, the improvement and depravation of our minds.

When you come into any company, observe their humours; suit your own carriage thereto, by which insinuation you will make their converse more free and open. Let your discourse be more in queries and doubtings, than peremptory assertions or disputings. *Newton.*

A man without complaisance ought to have a great deal of merit, in the room of it.

There are many arts of graciousness and conciliation which are to be practised without expence, and by which those may be made our friends, who have never received

ceived from us any real benefit. Such arts when they include neither guilt nor mean-nefs, it is furely reafonable to learn ; for who would want that love which is fo eafi-ly to be gained. *Johnfon.*

Our converfation fhould be fuch, that youth may therein find improvement, wo-men modefty, the aged refpect, and all men civility.

Talkativenefs is ufually called a feminine vice ; but it is poffible to go into mafculine company, where it will be as hard to wedge in a word as at a female goffiping.

He whofe honeft freedom makes it his virtue to fpeak what he thinks, makes it his neceffity to think what is good.

He that is peremptory in his own ftory, may meet with another that is peremptory in the contradiction of it, and then the two *fir pofitives* muft have a fkirmifh.

Victory ever inclines to him that con-tends the leaft.

Lefs pains a man cannot take, than to hold his tongue. Hear much and fpeak little ; for the tongue is the inftrument of the greateft good, and greateft evil, that is done in the world. *Raleigh.*

F 4

If

If any man offend thee with too much impertinent talk, do not give him the hearing, and that will be revenge enough.

Delight not thyself with lampoons, satires, and jests; for, whatever pleasure they procure at first, the reflection that follows, is rarely favorable to the author.

Raillery must be fine and delicate, and such as rather serves to heighten conversation, than offend the persons which compose the assembly.

Vile and debauched expressions are the sure marks of an abject and groveling mind, and the filthy overflowing of a vicious heart. *Spec.*

The hatred of the vicious will do you less harm than their conversation.

To inform, or to be informed, ought to be the end of all conferences. Men are too apt to be concerned for their credit, more than for the cause.

Some say, that hurt never comes by silence. But they may as well say, that good never comes by speech; for, where it is good to speak, it is ill to be silent.

Resolve to speak, and act well in company, in spite of those who do ill; whose vice,

vice, fet againft thy virtue, will render it the more confpicuous and excellent.

A quaint and folicitious way of fpeaking is the fign of a weak mind.

Freedom, which is the life of converfation, muft be reciprocal, or it cannot be agreeable.

We fhould always accommodate ourfelves to the capacity of thofe with whom we converfe. The difcourfe of fome men is as the ftars, which give light, becaufe they are fo high.

It is a great mafterpiece to fpeak well, without affecting knowledge.

Nothing requires more judgement than to rally inoffenfively, and to make this innocent war agreeable and pleafant.

He that is truly polite, knows how to contradict with refpect, and to pleafe without adulation; and is equally remote from an infipid complaifance, and a low familiarity.

It is a fure method of obliging in converfation, to fhow a pleafure in giving attention.

In difcourfe it is good to hear others firft; for filence has the fame effect as authority.

F 5 Better

Better fay nothing, than not to the purpofe; and, to fpeak pertinently, confider both what is fit, and when it is fit to fpeak.

Rhetoric in ferious difcourfes is like the flowers in corn; pleafing to thofe who come only for amufement, but prejudicial to him who would reap profit from it. *Swift.*

As men of fenfe fay a great deal in few words; fo the half-witted have a talent of talking much, and yet faying nothing.

If you think twice before you fpeak once, you will fpeak twice the better for it.

Contrive as much as you can beforehand of what to difcourfe; and lay your fcene, which afterward you may manage as you pleafe.

One reafon why we fee fo few agreeable in converfation, is, that almoft every body is more intent upon what he himfelf has a mind to fay, than upon making pertinent replies to what the reft of the company fay to him. *Rochef.*

He that talks all he knows, will talk more than he knows. Great talkers difcharge too thick to take always true aim.

To

To one you find full of queſtions, it is beſt to make no anſwer at all.

We ſometimes ſhall meet with a frothy wit, who would rather loſe his beſt friend, than his worſt jeſt.

Modeſty in your diſcourſe will give a luſtre to truth, and an excuſe to your error.

Your wit may make clear things doubtful; but it is your prudence to make doubtful things clear.

If your opinion be indefenſible, do not obſtinately maintain a bad cauſe. He that argues againſt truth, takes pains to be overcome.

We are not ſo much to regard who ſpeaks, as what is ſpoken.

In tabletalk, ſays *Montaigne*, I prefer the pleaſant and witty, before the learned and the grave.

Some men are ſilent for want of matter, or aſſurance; and ſome again are talkative for want of ſenſe.

It is a ſign of great prudence to be willing to receive inſtruction: the moſt intelligent perſon ſometimes ſtands in need of it.

To

To fpeak in fuperlatives falls fo much fhort of truth, as it goes beyond it.

A reproof has more effect when it comes by a fide-wind, than if it were levelled directly at a perfon.

There are braying men in the world, as well as braying affes; for what is loud and fenfelefs talking, huffing, and fwearing; any other than a more fafhionable way of braying ? *L'Eft.*

Too much affeveration gives ground of fufpicion. Truth and honefty have no need of loud proteftations.

The tongue is as a wild beaft, very difficult to be chained again, when once let loofe.

It was good advice given to one, not fo much as to laugh in compliance with him, that derides another; for you will be hated by him he derides.

We muft fpeak well, and act well. Brave actions are the fubftance of life, and good fayings the ornament of it.

He can never fpeak well, that can never hold his tongue. It is one thing to fpeak much, and another to fpeak pertinently. Much tongue and much judgment feldom go together; for talking and thinking are two quite different faculties; and there is commonly more depth, where there is less noise.

Some people write, and others talk themselves out of their reputation.

Conversation is generally confined on indifferent, low, or perhaps vicious subjects; and all that is serious or good, is almost banished the world. Some are so black in the mouth, as to utter nothing that is decent; supplying want of wit with want of modesty, and want of reputation with want of shame.

Buffoonery and scurrility are the corruption of wit, as knavery is of wisdom.

A jest, told in a grave manner, has the better effect; but you extinguish the appetite of laughing in others, if you prevent them by your own.

The spleen does sometimes great service in company; it makes illnature pass for ill health, dulness for gravity, and ignorance for reservedness.

He that can reply calmly to an angry man, is too hard for him.

A man, secluded from company, can have but the devil and himself to tempt him;

him; but he that converses much in the world, has almost as many snares as he has companions.

Good offices are the cement of society.

Casual omissions, and little sallies of heat or liberty should go for nothing.

A gentleman should talk like a gentleman; which is like a wise man.

At table (*it is a saying*) the company should never exceed that of the Muses, nor be under the number of the Graces.

Some, under a fool's cap, exercise a knave's wit: making a seeming simplicity the excuse of their impudence.

A too great credulity is great simplicity; and to believe nothing, because our narrow capacities cannot comprehend it, is great stupidity.

The life of life is society; of society, freedom; of freedom, the discreet and moderate use of it.

It is a fair step toward happiness and virtue, to delight in the conversation of good and wise men; and where that cannot be had, the next point is, to keep no company at all.

He

He who treats men ingenuously, and converses kindly with them, gains a good esteem with a very easy expence.

Goodnature is more agreeable in conversation than wit; and gives a certain air to the countenance, which is more amiable than beauty.

There is no man but delights to be questioned in his own profession; when, moved by others, he may seem to publish his knowledge without ostentation.

It is ungenerous to give a man occasion to blush at his own ignorance in any one thing, who perhaps may excel us in many.

Superlative commendations, beside bringing in question the sincerity of the speaker, often gives offence to the hearer, and do no credit to the person commended.

To have the reputation of a wit is but little credit, since it is generally applied rather to raillery and satire, than pregnancy and beauty of conceit.

Instructions are entertained with better effect, when they are not too personally addressed. We may with civility glance at, but cannot without rudeness and ill manners stare upon, the faults and imperfections of any man.

Discretion

Difcretion of fpeech is more than elo-quence; and to fpeak agreeable to him with whom we converfe, is more than to fpeak in exact order. *Bacon.*

The value of things is not in their fize, but quality; and fo of reafon, which, wrap-ped in few words, has the greater weight.

The greateft wifdom of fpeech is to know when, and what, and where to fpeak; the time, matter, manner: the next to it, is filence.

To ufe too many circumftances, before one comes to the matter, is wearifome; to ufe none, is blunt. *Bacon.*

Some are fo flow of fpeech and fo very dull, that their heads may be compared to an alembic, which gives you drop by drop an extract of the fimples in it. *Balz.*

It is common with fome men to fwear, only to fill up the vacuities of their empty difcourfe.

Common fwearing argues in a man a perpetual diftruft of his own reputation; and is an acknowledgment, that he thinks his bare word not to be worthy of credit. *Tillotf.*

That

That which is not fit to be practifed, is not fit to be fo much as mentioned.

Men are pleafed with a jefter, but never efteem him. A merry fellow is the faddeft fellow in the world. *Spec.*

You will never be thought to talk too much, when you talk well; and always fpeak too much, when you fpeak ill.

He that has a fatirical vein, as he makes others afraid of his wit, fo he had need be afraid of others memory. *Bacon.*

As a man fhould not conftrue that in earneft, which is fpoken in jeft, fo he fhould not fpeak that in jeft, which may be conftrued in earneft.

None, above the character of wearing a churlifh man's livery, ought to bear with his ill manners. *Spec.*

In reafoning, the beft way to carry the caufe, and which will bring the controverfy to a fpeedy determination, is by afking queftions, and proceeding ftill upon the adverfary's conceffion.

Words are the pledges and pictures of our thoughts; and therefore ought not to be obfcure and obfolete. Truth, as *Euripides* fays, loves plain language.

A man

A man may contemplate of virtue in folitude and retirement; but the practical part confifts in its participation, and the fociety it has with others; for whatfoever is good is the better for being communicable.

We learn more truth of ourfelves from our enemies than our friends.

The talent of turning men into ridicule, and expofing thofe we converfe with, is the qualification of little ungenerous tempers. The greateft blemifhes are often found in the moft fhining characters: but what an abfurd thing is it to pafs over all the valuable parts of a man, and fix our attention on his infirmities; to deferve his imperfections more than his virtues! *Spec.*

A little wit, and a great deal of illnature, will furnifh a man for fatire; but the greateft inftance of wit is to commend well. *Tillotf.*

Complaifance renders a fuperior amiable, an equal agreeable, and an inferior acceptable.

It is an excellent rule to be obferved in all difputes, that men fhould give foft words and hard arguments: that they fhould not fo much ftrive to vex, as to convince an enemy. *Wilkins.*

Contradiction

Contradiction fhould awaken our attention and care, but not our paffion; we muft be of no fide or intereft but that of truth.

Wherever the fpeech is corrupted, fo is the mind. *Sen.*

A great talker will always fpeak, though nobody minds him; nor does he mind any body when they fpeak to him.

Zeno, of all virtues, made his choice of filence: for by it, faid he, I hear other men's imperfections, and conceal my own.

Nothing is more filly than an ill-timed laugh. Many are feen to laugh at their own imperfections in another.

A jeft is no argument, nor a loud laughter a demonftration.

A man's attire, and exceffive laughter fhow what he is.

He that in company only ftudies men's diverfion, fhould be fure at the fame time to lofe their refpect. *Epict.*

A common fwearer has a brain without any idea on the fwearing fide. *Tat.*

The two frequent fafhion of oaths and imprecations has no temptation to excufe it, no man being born of a fwearing conftitution.

He

He that reveals a fecret, injures them to whom he tells it, as well as himfelf.   The beft maxim, concerning fecrets, is, neither to hear, nor to divulge them.

A gentle reply to fcurrilous language is the moft fevere revenge.

The deepeft waters are the moft filent; empty veffels make the greateft found, and tinkling cymbals the worft mufic.   They who think leaft, commonly fpeak moft. *Tat.*

The hearts of fools are in their mouths; but the tongues of the wife are in their hearts.

Silence is fometimes more fignificant and fublime, than the moft noble and moft expreffive eloquence.

Inftructive ridicule often does more than reprehenfion.

It was a good reproof of *Ariftotle*, to an egregious prater that had perplexed him with ma y abfurd ftories, concluded with this idle repetition, *And is not this a wonderful thing!* No wonder at all, faid *Ariftotle*, this; but, if a man fhould ftand ftill to hear you prate thus, that were a wonder indeed.

A conluding

A concluding face, put upon no concluding argument, is the moſt contemptible ſort of folly.

Metals are known by their weight, and men by their talk. Material gravity makes gold precious, and moral renders the man ſo.

To be reſerved in ſpeaking is the ſeal of the capacity. *Gracian.*

No injury makes ſo deep an impreſſion in one's memory, as that which is done by a cutting malicious jeſt; for, let it be ever ſo good, yet it is always extreme bad, when it occaſions enmity.

It is uſual with obſtinate perſons to regard neither truth in contradicting, nor benefit in diſputing. Poſitiveneſs is a certain evidence of a weak judgment.

A wellbred man, ſays *Montaigne,* is always ſociable and complaiſant.

Complaiſance obliges while it reprehends: without this the beſt advice ſeems but a reproach. Praiſe is diſagreeable, and converſation troubleſome.

They who have the true taſte of converſation, enjoy themſelves in communication of each other's excellencies, and not

in

in a triumph over their imperfections. *Spec.*

Too great a diſtruſt of one's ſelf produces a baſe fear, which, depriving our minds of their liberty and aſſurance, makes our reaſonings weak, our words trembling, and our actions faint.

The only way to be amiable is to be affable.

In converſation, a man of good ſenſe will ſeem to be leſs knowing, to be more obliging; and chooſe to be on a level with others, rather than oppreſs with the ſuperiority of his genius. *Tat.*

We are apt to fall into error, when we ſtudy too much to pleaſe; and the ſubject of our diſcourſe is often weakened by this too curious care to give it an agreeable variety, which would be more ſtrong, if it were more natural. We loſe what is ſolid, in too eager purſuit of what is ornamental.

In a ſpeech delivered in a public aſſembly, it is expected a man ſhould uſe all his reaſons in the caſe he handles: but in private perſuaſions it is a great error. *Bacon.*

Paſſionate diſputes darken our reaſon, but ſeldom enlighten our underſtanding.

If

If incivility proceeds from pride, it deserves to be hated; if from brutifhnefs, it is only contemptible. *Gracian.*

Excefs of ceremony fhows want of breeding. That civility is beft, which excludes all fuperfluous formality.

A tale out of feafon, is as mufic in mourning.

A good tale, ill told, is a bad one.

He that makes himfelf the common jefter of a company, has but juft wit enough to be a fool.

Sharp jefts are blunted more by neglecting, than by refponding, except they be fuddenly and wittily retorted.

Confine your tongue, left it confine you.

Such as hear difobliging difcourfe, and repeat it again to the perfons concerned, are much miftaken, if they think to oblige them by fuch indifcreet confidences.

Thofe that admonifh their friends, fays *Plutarch*, fhould obferve this rule, *not to leave them with fharp expreffions.* Ill language deftroys the force of reprehenfion, which fhould be always given with prudence and circumfpection.

Weak

Weak men are generally moſt loquacious, thinking to make up that in number of words, which is wanting in weight of argument.

In heat of argument, men are commonly like thoſe that are tied back to back; cloſe joined, and yet they cannot ſee one another.

Subtile diſputations are only the ſport of wits, and fitter to be contemned, than reſolved. *Sen.*

As, among wiſe men, he is the wiſeſt, that thinks he knows leaſt; ſo, among fools, he is the greateſt, that thinks he knows moſt.

Familiar converſation ought to be the ſchool of learning and good breeding. A man ought to make his maſters of his friends, ſeaſoning the pleaſure of converſe with the profit of inſtruction.

A good underſtanding, with a bad will, makes a very unhappy conjunction. That is an unlucky wit which is employed to do evil. Knowledge will become folly, if good ſenſe do not take care of it.

There is a time when nothing, a time when ſomething, but no time when all things are to be ſpoken.

It

It is beft mourning alone, and beft rejoicing in company.

It is obferved of the public and private life, that a man lives in one cafe to his country, in the other to himfelf. The one is a life of thought, the other of action; and both are prettily defined by an old philofopher: it is pleafant, faid *Ifocrates*, to be alone; and it is pleafant to be talking of it in good company; which comprifes the comforts of both conditions in one.

The true art of converfation feems to be this: an agreeable freedom and opennefs, wih a refervednefs as little appearing as is poffible. *Tillotf.*

This rule fhould be obferved in all converfation, *That men fhould not talk to pleafe themfelves, but thofe that hear them.* This would make them confider, whether what they fpeak be worth hearing? Whether there be either wit or fenfe in what they are about to fay? And whether it be adapted to the time when, the place where, and the perfon to whom it is fpoken? *Tat.*

Death and life are in the power of the tongue.

G   There

There are times in which the wife and the knowing are willing to receive praife, without the labour of deferving it, in which the moft elevated mind is willing to defcend, and the moft active to be at reft. All therefore are, at fome hour or another, fond of companions whom they can entertain upon eafy terms, and who will relieve them from folitude, without condemning them to vigilance and caution. *Johnfon.*

Let your fubject, fays *Epictetus,* be fomething of neceffity and ufe; fomething that may advance the love and practice of virtue, reform the paffions, or inftruct the underftanding; fuch as may adminifter advice to men in difficulties, comfort them under afflictions, affift them in the fearch of the truth, give them a reverent fenfe of God, and an awful admiration of his divine excellencies.

Of

Of the GENEROUS MIND.

MEN of the nobleſt diſpoſitions, think themſelves happieſt, when others ſhare with them in their happineſs. *Taylor*.

Goodnature is the very air of a good mind, the ſign of a large and generous ſoul, and the peculiar ſoil in which virtue proſpers.

It is according to nature to be merciful; for no man, that has not diveſted himſelf of humanity, can be hardhearted to others, without feeling a pain in himſelf.

Emulation is a noble paſſion, as it ſtrives to excel by raiſing itſelf, and not by depreſſing another.

There is far more ſatisfaction in doing, than receiving good. To relieve the oppreſſed is the moſt glorious act a man is capable of; it is, in ſome meaſure, doing the buſineſs of God and Providence; and is attended with a heavenly pleaſure, unknown but to thoſe that are beneficent and liberal. *Spec*.

True greatneſs of mind is to be maintained only by Chriſtian principles.

It

It is not in the power of a good man to refuse making another happy, where he has both ability and opportunity. *Spec.*

He that is senfible of no evil but what he feels, has a hard heart; and he that can spa e no kindnefs from himfelf, has a narrow foul.

Alphonfus, king of Sicily, being afked, what he would referve for himfelf, who gave fo much away, replied; Even thofe things that I give; for the reft I efteem as nothing.

Goodnefs is generous and diffufive; it is largenefs of mind, and fweetnefs of temper; modeft and fincere, inoffenfive and obliging. Where this quality is predominant, there is a noble forwardnefs for public benefit; an ardour to relieve the wants, to remove the oppreffions, and better the condition of all mankind. *Col.*

Liberality and thankfulnefs are the bonds of concord. *Cicero.*

No character is more glorious, none more attractive of univerfal admiration and refpect, than that of helping thofe who are in no condition of helping themfelves. *Char.*

Cefar ufed to fay, that no mufic was fo charming in his ears, as the requefts of his friends,

friends, and the fupplications of thofe in want of his affiftance.

By compaffion we make other's mifery our own; and fo, by relieving them, we at the fame time relieve ourfelves alfo. *Brown.*

It is better to be of the number of thofe who need relief, than of thofe who want hearts to give it.

Some who are reduced to the laft extremities, would rather perifh, than expofe their condition to any, fave the great and noble-minded. They efteem fuch to be wife men, generous, and confiderate of the accidents which commonly befal us. They think, to thofe they may freely unbofom themfelves, and tell their wants, without the hazard of a reproach, which wounds more deeply than a fhort denial. *Turk Spy.*

It was well faid of him, that called a good office, that was done harfhly, *A ftony piece of bread:* it is necffary for him that is hungry to receive it; but it almoft chokes him in the going down. *Sen.*

Auguftus received all fuitors with fuch great humanity, that he pleafantly rebuked one of them, becaufe in giving him his petition (he faid) he did it fo timoroufly,

G 3

as

as if he had been reaching meat to an elephant.

That which is given with pride and ostentation, is rather an ambition than a bounty. Let a benefit be ever so considerable, the manner of conferring it is yet the noblest part.

No object is more pleasing to the eye, than the sight of a man whom you have obliged; nor any music so agreeable to the ear, as the voice of one that owns you for his benefactor. *Spec.*

The qualifications which render men worthy of favours, are the same which make them desirous to acknowledge them. There may be as much generosity showed in the handsome acknowledgment of a kindness, as there is in conferring of that which deserves such acknowledgment.

It is a good rule for every one who has a competency of fortune, to lay aside a certain proportion of his income, for pious and charitable uses; he will then always give easily and cheerfully. *Spec.*

History reports of *Titus*, the son of *Vespasian*, that he never suffered a man to depart with discontent out of his presence.

It

It is part of a charitable man's epitaph, *What I poſſeſſed is left to others; what I gave away, remains with me.*

Anaxagoras, who had a large eſtate, gave the greateſt part of it to his friends; and, being blamed for his careleſſneſs, anſwered, It is enough for *you* to care. One aſking him, why he had no regard for his country? I have, ſaid he, and pointed toward heaven. When he returned home, after travel, and ſaw his former poſſeſſions, he ſaid, Had I not loſt theſe, I ſhould have been loſt myſelf. And, at the time he was dying, his friends aſking, where he would. be buried? No matter, ſaid he; there is a ſhort cut into the other world everywhere.

Mark Antony, when depreſſed, and at an ebb of fortune, cried out, That he had loſt all, except what he had given away.

Don Alphonſo, king of Naples, by alighting from his horſe to relieve a countryman that was in danger, gained the city of Gæta in a few hours, by making his firſt entry at their hearts, which the battery of his guns could not have done in many days.

Cyrus, the firſt emperor of Perſia, obtained a victory over the Aſſyrians; and,

G 4

after

after the battle, was so sensibly touched with seeing the field covered with dead bodies, that he ordered the same care to be taken of the wounded Assyrians, as of his own soldiers, saying, They are men as well as we, and are no longer enemies, when once they are vanquished.

Rutilus was told in his exile, that for his comfort there would be, ere long, a civil war, which would bring all the banished men home again. God forbid! said he; for I had rather my country should blush for my banishment, than mourn for my return.

Caius, a nobleman of Rome, who was thrice consul; when he had beaten *Pyrrhus*, king of Epirus, and drove him out of Italy, he divided the land, distributing to every man four acres, and reserved no more for himself; saying, That none ought to be a general, who could not be content with a common soldier's share; and that he had rather rule over rich men, than be rich himself.

Sesostris, king of Egypt, having his chariot drawn by four kings, who were his captives, one of them had his eye continually on the chariot wheel: whereupon *Sesostris* asked, What he meant by it? He answered,

As

As often as I behold the turning of the wheel (in which that part which is now lowest is presently highest, and the highest presently lowest) it puts me in mind of our fortune. Whereat *Sesostris* being moved, gave them their liberty.

The words of *Lewis* XII of France, showed a great and noble mind; who being advised to punish those that had wronged him before he was king, answered; It is not becoming a king of France to avenge injuries done to a duke of Orleans.

He that is noble-minded, has the same concern for his own fortune, that every wise man ought to have, and the same regard for his friend, that every good man really has. His easy graceful manner of obliging carries as many charms as the obligation itself: his favours are not extorted from him by importunity; are not the late rewards of long attendance and expectation; but flow from a free hand and open heart.

A man advanced to greatness, who makes others find their fortune in his, joins a great merit to a great happiness. *St. Evr.*

There is no character more deservedly esteemed, than that of a country gentleman, who understands the station in which hea-

ven

ven and nature have placed him. He is a father to his tenants, a patron to his neighbours, and is more superior to thofe of lower fortune, by his benevolence, than his poffeffions. He juftly divides his time between folitude and company; fo as to ufe the one for the other: his life is employed in the good offices of an advocate, a referee, a companion, a mediator, and a friend. *Spec.*

It was a faying of *Pliny*, that he efteemed him the beft good man, that forgave others, as if he were every day faulty himfelf; and who abftained from faults, as if he pardoned nobody.

Goodnefs of nature is of all virtues and dignities of the mind the greateft, being the character of the deity; and without it man is a bufy, mifchievous, wretched thing, no better than a kind of vermin. *Bacon.*

Of BENEFITS, GRATITUDE, and INGRATITUDE.

THERE is no vice or failing of man doth unprinciple humanity, like ingratitude; since he who is guilty of it, lives unworthy of his soul, that has not virtue enough to be obliged, or to acknowledge the due merits of the obliger.

Ingratitude is, of all crimes, that which we are to account the most venial in others, and the most unpardonable in ourselves. *Sen.*

Gratitude is a duty none can be excused from, because it is always in our own disposal. *Char.*

The ungrateful, says *Xenophon*, are neither fit to serve the gods, their country, nor their friends.

Without goodnature and gratitude, men had as well live in a wilderness, as in a civil society.

He who conceals a benefit, is to be held but one degree from denying it.

G 6   It

It was a great commendation of the *Lacedemonians*, that they knew how to give, and to receive, prudently.

Friendſhip is a medicine for all misfortune: but ingratitude dries up the fountain of all goodneſs. *Richl.*

Ingratitude is directly oppoſite to nature and equity, it is hardly known among brutes; for benefits and kindneſs have mollified lions.

It is as common a thing for gratitude to be forgetful, as for hope to be mindful. When once a man has drank, he turns his back upon the well.

He that receives a benefit without being thankful, robs the giver of his juſt reward. It muſt be a due reciprocation in virtue, that can make the obliger and the obliged worthy.

To make too much haſte to return an obligation, is a ſort of ingratitude. *Rochef.*

He who receives a good turn, ſhould never forget it: he who does one, ſhould never remember it. *Char.*

To refuſe a good office, not ſo much becauſe we do not need it, as becauſe we would not be indebted for it, is a kind of fantaſtical ingratitude. *Sen.*

Cato

Cato boasts of this as the great comfort and joy of his old age, That nothing was more pleasant to him, than the conscience of a well spent life, and the remembrance of many benefits and kindnesses done to others.

It is the character of an unworthy nature to write injuries in marble, and benefits in dust.

He that preaches gratitude, pleads the cause both of God and man; for without it we can be neither sociable, nor religious. *Sen.*

So long as we stand in need of a benefit, there is nothing dearer to us; nor any thing cheaper, when we have received it.

It is the glory of gratitude, that it depends only on the will: If I have a will to be grateful, says *Seneca*, I am so.

An anticipated favour has two perfections: one is the promptitude of it, which obliges the receiver to greater gratitude; and the other, in that the same gift, which coming later, would be a debt, by anticipation is a pure benefit.

OF

Of HONOURS, and of the GREAT.

TRUE honour, as defined by *Cicero*, is *the concurrent approbation of good men*; such only being fit to give true praise, who are themselves praiseworthy.

Anciently the *Romans* worshipped Virtue and Honour for gods; whence it was that they built two temples, which were so seated, as none could enter the temple of Honour, without passing through the temple of Virtue.

No man can be great, says *Longinus*, by being owner of those things which wise men have always counted it a piece of greatness to despise. It is not the possession, but the right management of any valuable advantage, which makes us considerable.

Nobility is to be considered only as an imaginary distinction, unless accompanied with the practice of those generous virtues by which it ought to be obtained. Titles of honour, conferred upon such as have no personal merit to deserve them, are at best but the royal stamp set upon base metal. *Tat.*

The

The way to be truly honoured is to be illuſtriouſly good. It was worthily anſwered by *Maximilian*, the German emperor, to one who deſired his letters-patent to ennoble him; I am able (ſaid he) to make thee rich; but virtue muſt make thee noble.

Great qualities make great men. Who, ſays *Seneca*, is a gentleman? The man, whom nature has diſpoſed, and as it were cut out for virtue; this man is well born indeed; for he wants nothing elſe to make him noble, who has a mind ſo generous, that he can riſe above, and triumph over fortune, let his condition of life be what it will.

It is true greatneſs that conſtitutes glory, and virtue is the cauſe of both : but vice and ignorance taint the blood; and an unworthy behaviour degrades and diſennobles a man more than birth and fortune aggrandize and exalt him. *Guard*.

Virtue is the ſureſt foundation both of reputation and fortune, and the firſt ſtep to greatneſs is to be honeſt. *Johnſon*.

He that boaſts of his anceſtors, confeſſes he has no virtue of his own. No other peiſon has lived for our honour; nor ought that to be reputed ours, which was long before we had a being : for what advantage

vantage can it be to a blind man, that his parents had good eyes.   *Char.*

It was a fine compliment made to the emperor *Vespasian:* Greatness and majesty have changed nothing in you but this, that your power to do good should be answerable to your will.

The world is a theatre; the best actors are those that represent their parts most naturally; but the wisest are seldom the heroes in the play. It is not to be considered, says *Epictetus,* who is prince, or who is beggar; but who acts the prince, or the beggar, best.

It is mentioned in history to the honour of the emperor *Alexander Severus,* that he would in no case permit offices to be sold: For, said he, he who buys must sell: I will not indure any merchandise of authority, which, if I tolerate, I cannot afterward condemn; and I shall be ashamed to punish him who sold what I permitted him to buy.

Men must have public minds, as well as salaries; or they will serve private ends at the public cost.   It was Roman virtue, that raised the Roman glory.

It

It was a saying of *Bias*, Magiftracy difcovers what a man is. For as empty veffels, though they have fome crack in them, while they are empty, do not difcover their flaws; but, when they are filled with liquor, immediately fhow their defects; fo happens it with ill-difpofed and corrupt minds, which feldom difcover their vices, till they are filled with authority.

A hero fhould have all good qualities united in him, without affecting any. For what need has a great man of any foreign aid to promote the regard that is due to his merit, when a certain air of noble fimplicity, and forgetfulnefs of his own grandeur, will not fail to attach the public attention; fince fhutting his eyes upon himfelf is an infallible way to open all the world's upon him ? *Gracian*.

If favour places a man above his equals, his fall places him below them.

It is a fhame for a man of honour and good fenfe to ftay waiting at courts, when the end of his fervices is become the end of his intereft and merit. As for myfelf, fays *St. Evremond*, I fhould rather choofe to live in a convent or defart, than occafion, in thofe that are my friends, compaffion;

and,

and, in thofe that are not, the malicious
pleafure of raillery.

It is with followers at court, as with followers on the road, who firft difpatter thofe
that go before, and then tread on their heels.
Swift.

The prepoffeffions of the vulgar for men
in power and authority are fo blind, and
they are generally fo admired in every thing
they do, that if they could bethink themfelves of being good, the multitude would
in a manner idolife them. But, as *Gracian*
obferves, when excellence concurs with
high birth and fortune, it paffes for a pro-
digy.

The greater a man is in power above
others, the more he ought to excel them in
virtue : wherefore *Cyrus* faid, That none
ought to govern, who was not better than
thofe he governed.

He that becomes acquainted and is in-
vefted with authority and influence, will
in a fhort time be convinced, that in proportion as the power of doing well is en-
larged, the temptations to do ill are mul-
tiplied and enforced. *Johnfon.*

All things have fome kind of ftandard,
by which the natural goodnefs of them is
to be meafured. We do not therefore
esteem

efteem a fhip to be good, becaufe it is curi-oufly carved, painted, and gilded; but be-caufe it is fitted for all the purpofes of navi-gation, which is the proper end of a fhip. It would be fo likewife in our efteem of men, who are not fo much to be valued for the grandeur of their eftates or titles, as by their inward goodnefs and excellence. *Sen.*

That which I admire at moft in the for-tune of great men, fays *Montaigne*, is the crowd of their adorers. All fubmiffion is due to kings, but that of the underftanding; my reafon is not obliged to bow and bend, though my knees are.

It is not, it feems, within the rules of good breeding, to tax the vices of perfons of quality; as if the commandments were made only for the vulgar. *Addif.*

He that depends wholly upon the worth of others, ought to confider, that he has but the honour of an image; and is wor-fhipped, not for his own fake, but upon the account of what he reprefents. It is a fign a man is very poor, when he has no-thing of his own to appear in, but is forced to patch up his figure with the relics of the dead, and rifle tomb-ftones and monuments for reputation.

What

What is truly great and majeſtic, looks more like itſelf, the leſs it is adorned. I ſtudy to make my life famous, ſaid king *Theſeus*, not ſo much by ſplendid appearances, and the applauſes of others, as by my own acts of ſolid virtue.

Let any one remove his eye from the moſt magnificent parade, or triumph, to the expanſe of heaven; and inſtantly, what was great is little, what was public is private. *Young.*

A difficult acceſs is the vice of thoſe, whoſe manners, honour and preferment have changed. Few perſons in high employments retain the virtues of their private condition: but it argues men do not deſerve great places, when they can value themſelves upon them.

It is not the place, ſays *Cicero*, that makes the perſon, but the perſon that makes the place honorable.

Nothing is more odious than the practice of thoſe great men, who with fine looks and promiſes make one hope for ſervices they never mean to perform. *Find out ſomething wherein I can ſerve you,* ſays a court minion; and then, upon the diſcovery, he lays hold on it to ſome other purpoſe. *L'Eſtr.*

Great

Great men are generally for making what they do real favours; for, fhould they prefer the deferving only; it would be like paying a debt, not doing a favour.

No government can flourifh, where the morals and manners of the people are corrupted: for, as *Tully* obferves, take but away the awe of religion, all that fidelity and juftice, fo neceffary to the keeping up human fociety, muft perifh with it.

The beft inftruments of good government are good counfellors. He that is not wife of himfelf, can never be well counfelled.

Paffive obedience, unlimited power, and indefeafible right, feem to have fomething of a venerable meaning in them; whereas in reality they only imply, that a king has a right to be a tyrant; and that the people are obliged in confcience to be flaves. *Addif.*

The *Rabbins* had a faying, that if the fea was ink, and the earth parchment, they would not be fufficient to defcribe and contain the praifes of liberry.

Who could have greater honour than *Agefilaus* king of Sparta had, who was fined by the *Ephori* for having ftolen the hearts of the people to himfelf? Of whom it is said,

said, that he ruled his country by obeying it.

Henry III, of France, afking thofe about him, what it was that the duke of Guife did to charm and allure every one's heart; received this anfwer: Sire, the duke de Guife does good to all the world, without exception, either directly by himfelf or indirectly by his recommendations: he is civil, courteous, liberal: has always fome good to fay of every body, but never fpeaks evil of any: and this is the reafon he reigns in mens hearts, as abfolutely as your majefty does in your kingdom.

Though a honorable title may be conveyed to pofterity, yet the ennobling qualities which are the foul of greatnefs, are a fort of incommunicable perfections, and cannot be transferred. Indeed, if a man could bequeath his virtues by will, and fettle his fenfe and learning upon his heirs, as certainly as he can his lands, a brave anceftor would be a mighty privilege. *Col.*

Title and anceftry render a good man more illuftrious, but an ill one more contemptible. Vice is infamous, though in a prince, and virtue honorable, though in a peafant. *Addif.*

The

The *Athenians* raifed a noble ftatue to the memory of *Efop*, and placed a flave on a pedeftal, that men might know the way to honour was open to all.

Men in former ages, though fimple and plain, were great in themfelves, and independent on a thoufand things, which are fince invented to fupply perhaps that true greatnefs, which is now extinct. *Bruyere.*

There is a nobility without heraldry. Though I want the advantage of a noble birth, faid *Marius*, yet my actions afford me a greater one; and they who upbraid me with it, are guilty of an extreme injuftice, in not permitting me to value myfelf upon my own virtue, as much as they value themfelves upon the virtue of others. *Salluft.*

The *man* of honour is an internal, the *perfon* of honour is an external; the one a real, the other a fictitious character. A *perfon* of honour may be a profane libertine, penurious, proud; may infult his inferiors, and defraud his creditors; but it is impoffible for a *man* of honour to be guilty of any of thefe.

There is no true glory, no true greatnefs, without virtue; without which we do
but

but abuse all the good things we have, whether they be great or little; false or real. Riches make us either covetous or prodigal: fine palaces make us despise the poor and poverty: a great number of domestics flatter human pride, which uses them like slaves: and a high pedigree makes a man take up with the virtues of his ancestors, without endeavouring to acquire any himself. *Scudery*.

Honours are in this world under no regulation; true quality is neglected; virtue is oppressed, and vice triumphant. The last day will rectify this disorder, and assign to every one a station suitable to the dignity of his character; ranks will then be adjusted, and precedency set right. *Addis.*

OF

Of MERIT and REPUTATION, PRAISE, and FLATTERY.

THERE are few perfons to be found, but are more concerned for the reputation of wit and fenfe, than honefty and virtue. *Spec.*

He that fets no value upon a good repute, is as carelefs of the actions that produce it.

A man that is defirous to excel, fhould endeavour it in thofe things that are in themfelves moft excellent. *Epict.*

There is fcarce any man fo perfect, but we fhall find, that he has his weakneffes, which level him with the vulgar, as much as his merit raifes him above them.

Merit muft take a great compafs to rife, if not affifted by favour.

Fame is like a river, that bears up things light, and drowns thofe that are weighty and folid. *Bacon.*

The coin that is moft current among mankind, is *flattery:* the only benefit of which is, that, by hearing what we are not, we may be inftructed what we ought to be.

H   For

For people of worth, it is not neceffary to fetch praifes from their predeceffors; it is enough to fpeak of their own particular merit. It is happy to have fo much merit, that our birth is the leaft thing refpected in us.

We fhould be careful to deferve a good reputation, by doing well; and, when that care is once taken, not to be over anxious about the fuccefs. *Rochef.*

Nothing finks a greater character fo much as raifing it above credibility.

Princes are feldom dealt truly with, but when they are taught to ride the great horfe; which, knowing nothing of diffembling, will as foon throw an emperor as a groom.

No man fhould be confident of his own merit. The beft err, and the wifeft are deceived.

Our good qualities often expofe us to more hatred and perfecution, than all the ill we do.

The real fatisfaction which praife can afford, is when what is repeated aloud, agrees with the whifpers of confcience, by fhewing us that we have not endeavoured to deferve well in vain. *Johnfon.*

Praife

Praise from the common people is gene-rally false, and rather follows vain persons than virtuous. *Bacon.*

The common people are but ill judges of a man's merits; they are slaves to fame; their eyes are dazzled with the pomp of titles, large retinue, &c. and then no wonder, if they bestow their honours on those who least deserve them.

He that will sell his fame, will also sell the public interest. *Solon.*

Fame and conscience are of two different properties; the one blazes a man's deserts, yet makes him nothing the better; the other the better, yet never the more renowned.

Wherever there is flattery, there is al-ways a fool in the case: if the parasite be detected, it falls to his share; if he be not, to his whom he deludes.

It is frequent with many, upon every tri-vial matter, to pawn their reputation: a most inconsiderate thing! For what is so often lent, and passes so many hands upon every occasion, cannot but lose much of its value.

Great and good men will rather look for their characters in the writings and pre-cepts of philosophers, than in the hyperboles

of

of flatterers; for they know very well, that wise books are always true friends.

Little wit serves to flatter with; for how easily do they work, that go with the grain!

Fame is as difficult to be preserved, as it was at first to be acquired.   *Spec.*

It is a maxim of *Cato*'s, that a man ought to respect himself, *i. e.* respect his reason, that recommends a honest boldness, and forbids a servile fear, which is a kind of licence and permission for others to have no regard and consideration for us.

If we would perpetuate our fame or reputation, we must do things worth writing, or write things worth reading.   *Pliny.*

There are two sorts of enemies inseparable from almost all men, but altogether of men of great fortunes; the *flatterer* and the *liar:* one strikes before, the other behind; both insensibly, both dangerously.

No species of falsehood is more frequent than flattery, to which the coward is betayed by fear, the dependent by interest, and the friend by tenderness.   *Johnson.*

Some men think they can never set a just value on themselves, without the unjust

contempt

contempt of others; and yet will perform all acts of the moſt ſupererogating civility to thoſe above them; which is generally made up of ſuch hollow profeſſions, ſuch groſs flatteries, as are worſe than reproaches.

He that rebukes a man, ſhall afterward find more favour, than he that flatters with his tongue.

Men are not to be judged by their looks, habits, and appearances; but by the cha-racter of their lives and converſations, and by their works. It is better that a man's own works, than that another man's words, ſhould praiſe him. *L'Eſtr.*

When commended, examine impartially your own deſerts; and if you find not what is ſaid, note that tongue for the inſtrument of flattery. Know thyſelf, ſaid *Bias*; ſo ſhall no flatterer deceive thee.

Many take leſs care of their conſcience than their reputation. The religious man fears, the man of honour ſcorns to do an ill action.

Satisfaction can no where be placed but in a juſt ſenſe of our own integrity, without regard to the opinion of others. *Tat.*

H 3 Reputation

Reputation is often got without merit, and loſt without a crime.

It is ſaid of *Agricola*, that he never gloried in any thing he did; but, as an agent, referred the good ſucceſs of his fortune to the perſon that employed him; and ſo by his diſcretion and modeſty freed himſelf from envy, and loſt no part of his deſerved praiſe.

It is a thing exceding rare to diſtinguiſh virtue, and fortune. The moſt impious if proſperous, are always applauded; the moſt virtuous, if unproſperous, are ſure to be deſpiſed. *Spec.*

There is no ſuch flatterer, as is a man's ſelf; and there is no ſuch remedy againſt flattery of a man's ſelf, as the liberty of a friend. *Bacon.*

The flatterer is not often detected; for a honeſt mind is not apt to ſuſpect, and no one exerts the power of diſcernment with much vigour when ſelf-love favours the deceit. *Johnſon.*

I frequent the company more of thoſe who find fault with me, ſays *Montaigne,* than thoſe that flatter me; and am more proud of a conqueſt gained over myſelf, when I ſubmit to the force of my adverſary's reaſon, than I am pleaſed with a victory

tory obtained over him by reason of his weakness.

·There are no snares so dangerous as those that are laid for us under the name of good offices. The Greeks said, that flatterers never lift a man up, but as the eagle does the tortoise, to get something by his fall.

The philosopher *Bias*, being asked, what animal he thought the most hurtful? replied, that of wild creatures, a *tyrant*; and of tame ones, a *flatterer*.

Men of mean qualities show but little favour to great virtues. A lofty wisdom offends an ordinary reason.

Superiority in virtue is the most unpardonable provocation that can be given to a base mind. Innocence is too amiable to be beheld without hatred; and it is a secret acknowledgement of merit, which the wicked are betrayed into, when they pursue good men with violence. This behaviour visibly proceeds from a consciousness in them, that other people's virtue upbraids their own want of it.

It was said of the good emperor *Severus*, as well as of *Augustus*, that he should never have been born, or that he never should have died.

King *Alphonfus* was wont to fay, that his dead counfellors, *meaning his books*, were to him far better than the living; for they, without flattery or fear, prefented to him truth.

What is public efteem, but the opinion of many men in general, who are not much valued in particular? The judgment which the world makes of us, is of no manner of ufe to us; it adds nothing to our fouls or bodies, nor leffens any of our miferies. Let us conftantly follow reafon, fays *Montaigne*; and let the public approbation follow us the fame way if it pleafes.

How fatirical is that praife, which commends a man for virtues, that all the world knows he has not! Exceffive praifes excite curiofity, and incite to envy; fo that if merit anfwer not the value that is fet upon it (as it commonly happens) general opinion revolts from the impoftor, and makes the flatterer and flattered both ridiculous.

There is this good in commendation, that it helps to confirm men in the practice of virtue. No obligation can be of more force, than to render to eminent virtue its due merits.

The character of the perfon who commends you, is to be confidered, before you

set

fet a value upon his efteem. The wife man applauds him whom he thinks moft virtuous; the reft of the world him who is moft wealthy. *Spec.*

It is better, faid *Antifthenes*, to fall among crows, than flatterers; for thofe only devour the dead, thefe the living.

When the *Athenians* pulled down the ftatues of *Demetrius Phalerius*, They cannot, he faid, deprive me of thofe virtues that caufed them to be erected.

It is very ftrange, that no eftimate is made of any creature, except ourfelves, but by its proper qualities. He has a magnificent houfe, or fo many thoufand pounds a year, is the common way of eftimating men; though thefe things are only about them, not in them, and make no part of their character. *Mont.*

It was elegantly faid in a letter to cardinal *Richlieu*—My lord, as there was heretofore a valiant man who could not receive any wounds, but on the fcars of thofe he had already received; fo you cannot be praifed, but by repetitions: feeing that truth, which has its bounds, has faid for you, whatever falfehood, which knows no bounds, has invented for others.

H 5

Pythagoras

Pythagoras ufed to fay, that thofe who reproved us, were greater friends to us, than thofe who flattered us.

Fortune and futurity are not to be gueffed at; and fame does not always ftand upon defert and judgment. *Antoninus.*

Flatter not, nor be thou flattered. Follow the dictates of your reafon, and you are fafe.

Felicity confifts not in having the applaufe of the people at one's entrance; for that is an advantage, which all that enter, have: the difficulty is, to have the fame applaufe at one's exit.

A deathbed flattery is the worft of treacheries. Ceremonies of mode and compliment are mightily out of feafon, when life and falvation come to be at ftake. *L'Eftr.*

Honours, monuments, and all the works of vanity and ambition, are demolifhed and deftroyed by time; but the reputation of wifdom is venerable to pofterity. *Sen.*

Of

Of WEALTH, LUXURY, and the PURSUIT of PLEASURES.

NOTHING can be more inglorious, than a gentleman only by name; whose soul is ignorant, and life immoral. *Spec.*

Wisdom is better without an inheritance, than an inheritance without wisdom.

He that gets an estate, will keep it better than he that finds it.

Riches cannot purchase worthy endowments; they make us neither more wise, nor more healthy. None but intellectual possessions are what we can properly call our own. *Spec.*

It is observed of gold by an old epigrammatist, that to have it is to be in fear, and to want it, to be in sorrow.

Some people are nothing else but money, pride, and pleasure: these three things ingross their thoughts, and take up the whole soul of them. *Col.*

There is more money idly spent to be laughed at, than for any one thing in the world,

world, though the purchafers do not think fo. *Halifax.*

Too much wealth is generally the occafion of poverty. He whom the wantonnefs of abundance has once foftened, eafily finks into neglect of his affairs; and he that thinks he can afford to be negligent, is not far from being poor. *Johnfon.*

To keep a full table is a way to extend one's acquaintance, but no fure one to procure friends. Feafting makes no friendfhip.

All worldly pleafure is correfpondent to a like meafure of anxiety.

A great fortune in the hands of a fool is a great misfortune. The more riches a fool has, the greater fool he is.

Not to defire pleafures is equivalent to the enjoyment of them. I fee no greater pleafure in this world, faid *Tertullian*, than the contempt of pleafure.

It is remarkable, that among thofe that place their happinefs in fenfe, they are the moft miferable that feem to be the happieft. *Sen.*

How defpicable is his condition, who is above neceffity, and yet fhall refign his reafon, son, and his integrity, to purchase superfluities! *Tat.*

The luxurious live to eat and drink; but the wise and temperate eat and drink to live. *Plut.*

Cookery is now become so mysterious a trade, that the kitchen has almost as many intricacies as the schools. To keep the kitchen always hot, is the way to set the house on fire.

Those who live magnificently, for the most part, are the real poor; they endeavour to get money on all hands with disquiet and trouble, to maintain the pleasures of others. *St. Evr.*

Among the ancient *Romans,* there was a law kept inviolably, that no man should make a public feast, except he had before provided for all the poor of his neighbourhood.

The more servants a man keeps, the more spies he has upon him. That any man should make work for so many, or rather keep them from work, to make up a train, has a levity and luxury in it very surprising.

Democritus laughed at the whole world, but at nothing more in it, than people's eager pursuit of riches and honour.

Vice

Vice is covered by wealth, and virtue by poverty. *Spec.*

It is more honorable not to have, and yet deserve; than to have, and not deserve.

The little value Providence sets on riches, is seen by the persons, on whom they are generally bestowed. *Tat.*

He that is violent in the pursuit of pleasure, will not stick to turn villain for the purchase. *Antoninus.*

It is commonly seen, that the more mankind are favoured with the gifts of fortune, the less they are disposed to assist those that are destitute.

The fine gentlemen of this age are distinguished for their pride, luxury, and hardness of heart; they are utter strangers to compassion and humanity. *Spec.*

The *Man of Pleasure*, as the phrase is, is the most ridiculous of all beings: he travels, indeed, with his riband, plume, and bells; his dress, and his music; but through a toilsome and beaten road; and every day nauseously repeats the same tract. *Young.*

He that abounds in riches, good cheer, dogs, horses, equipages, fools, and flatterers,

flatterers, muſt certainly be a great man. *Bruyere.*

Wealth cannot confer greatneſs; for nothing can make that great, which the decree of nature has ordained to be little. The bramble may be placed in a hotbed, but can never become an oak. *Johnſon.*

Pray, what was you made for? (ſays the emperor *Antoninus*) for your pleaſures? Common ſenſe will not bear ſo ſcandalous an anſwer.

The little ſoul that converſes no higher than the looking-glaſs, and a fantaſtic dreſs, may help to make up the ſhow of the world; but muſt not be reckoned among the rational inhabitants of it.

How wretched is it to conſider the care and coſt laid out upon luxury and ſhow; and the general neglect of thoſe ſhining habits of the mind, which ſhould ſet us off in real and ſolid excellencies! When pleaſure is predominant, all virtues of courſe are excluded.

The memory of good and worthy actions gives a quicker reliſh to the ſoul, than ever it could poſſibly take in the higheſt enjoyments of youth. *Spec.*

If

If senfuality were pleafure, beafts are happier than men. But human felicity is lodged in the foul, not in the flesh.

Nature has cut off the coft and luxurious impertinencies of our affections, in food, raiment, and the like; in being contented, that her neceffities fhould be cheaply fupplied.

He that lives in pleafure, is dead while he lives; but he that refifts pleafures, crowns his life.

Let pleafures be ever fo innocent, the excefs is always criminal. *St. Evr.*

Who can help reflecting on thofe whofe tables are daily fpread to the fecond and third courfes, which kill many with furfeits, while as many ftarve at their gates with famine ?

He has riches fufficient, who has enough to be charitable. *Brown.*

The neceffities of the body are the proper meafure of our care for the things of this life; but if we once leave this rule, and exceed thofe neceffities, then are we carried into all the extravagancies in the world. *Epict.*

Pleafures

Pleafures unduly taken enervate the foul, make fools of the wife, and cowards of the brave.   A libertine life is not a life of liberty.

It was a fine anfwer of *Diogenes*, who being afked in mockery, why philofophers were the followers of rich men, and not rich men of philofophers; replied, becaufe the one knew what they had need of, and the other did not.

Though want is the fcorn of every wealthy fool, an innocent poverty is yet preferable to all the guilty affluence the world can offer.   *Tat.*

There cannot be a more ridiculous folly, than to fpend high, in confidence of reverfions, and diftant expectations.   *Char.*

Ariftotle wondered at nothing more than at this, that they were thought richer who had fuperfluous things, than they who had what were profitable and neceffary.

From the manner of mens bearing their condition, we often pity the profperous, and admire the unfortunate.   *Spec.*

So ftupid and brutifh, fo worthlefs and fcandalous, are too many feen in this degenerate age, that grandeur and equipage are looked upon as more indifpenfable than charity;

charity; and thofe creatures, which contribute merely to our pomp, or our diverfion, are more tenderly and fumptuoufly maintained, than fuch as are in neceffity among ourfelves.

Thofe perfons, fays *Tacitus*, are under a mighty error, who know not how to diftinguifh between liberality aud luxury. Abundance of men know how to fquander that do not know how to give.

Caligula made himfelf ridiculous by the foftnefs and fantafticalnefs of his habit; and *Auguftus* was as much admired for the modefty and gravity of his.

We are come to fuch an extraordinary pitch of politenefs, that the affectation of being gay, and in fafhion, has very near taken from us our good fenfe, and our religion.

The *vain* is the moft diftinguifhed fon of folly. In what does this man lay out the faculties of an immortal foul? That time, on which depends eternity? That eftate, which, well difpofed of, might, in fome meafure, purchafe heaven? What is his ferious labour, fubtile machination, ardent defire, and reigning ambition?—*To be feen.*
This

This ridiculous, but true anfwer, renders all grave cenfure almoft fuperfluous. *Young.*

What if a body might have all the pleafures in the world for the afking? Who would fo unman himfelf, as, by accepting of them, to defert his foul, and become a perpetual flave to his fenfes? *Sen.*

The delicacies of entertainments, the divertifements of the theatre, the magnificence of courts, nor the moft fhining affemblies, can give full fatisfaction to any wife man. *St. Evr.*

All worldly happinefs confifts in opinion.

There are too many of that unthinking temper of mind which troubles itfelf with nothing that is ferious and weighty; but account life a paftime, and feek nothing above recantation, never reflecting where all this will end at laft.

The temperate man's pleafures are durable, becaufe they are regular; and all his life is calm and ferene, becaufe it is innocent.

Pleafures, while they flatter a man, fting him to death.

A Felicity

A felicity, that cofts pain, gives double content.

Ariftippus faid, he liked no pleafure, but that which concerned a man's true happinefs.

The Greeks and Romans had in detefta-tion the very name of *Philoxenus*, for his filthy wifh of a crane's neck, for the plea-fure he took in eating.

Men may furfeit with too much, as well as ftarve with too little.

What is a man the worfe for the laft year's plain diet; or what now the better for the laft great feaft? What is a voluptu-ous dinner, and the frothy vanity of dif-courfe, that commonly attends thefe pomp-ous entertainments ? What is it but a mortification to a man of fenfe and vir-tue, to fpend his time among fuch people ? *L'Eftr.*

The fumptuous fideboard to an ingenu-ous eye has more the air of an altar, than a table.

He that looks into the offices of the luxu-rious, and fees the troops of fervants fweat-ing and hurrying up and down, the maf-facre of beafts and fowls, and every thing afloat in the richeft wine, cannot but won-

der

der at fo horrible a profufion for the guts of one family. *Bona.*

The *Egyptians* at their feafts, to prevent exceffes, fet a *fkeleton* before their guefts, with this motto, Remember *ye* muft be fhortly fuch.

Pleafures do but weaken our minds, and fend us for our fupport to Fortune, who gives us money only as the wages of flavery. *Sen.*

How ridiculous a fight is a vain young gallant, that briftles with his plumes, and fhakes his giddy head, and to no other purpofe, but to get poffeffion of a miftrefs, as very a trifle as himfelf!

We have worn out our virtues, and our vices have worn out us.

Some fo affect to be fingular, and to be known by their vices, that they feek out novelty in wickednefs, and glory in a bad reputation: or (as *Tacitus* obferves) find an exquifite pleafure, even in the grandeur of infamy.

No good man was ever inwardly troubled for the omiffion of any pleafures; from whence it follows, that pleafures, ftrictly fpeaking, are neither profitable nor good. *Antoninus.*

The

The tempers of some are so solid, and their constitutions so sedentary, that they cannot relish activity, or rough exercise: their very diversions are in a manner, contemplative, and bent on speculation : therefore they require amusements of a more refined nature.

There is but one solid pleasure in life; and that is our duty.   How miserable then, how unwise, how unpardonable are they, who make that one a pain !   *Young.*

All the treasures of the earth are not to be compared to the least virtue of the soul. *Socrates.*

A wicked man can never be happy, though he had the riches of *Crœsus*, the empire of *Cyrus*, and the glory of *Alexander*.   Wealth and honours can never cure a wounded conscience.

The consideration of the dignity and excellency of our nature plainly informs us, how mean and unworthy it is to dissolve in luxury, softness, and effeminacy; and how becoming it is, on the other hand, to lead a life of frugality, temperance, and sobriety. *Cicero.*

Some by wit may get wealth; but none by wealth can purchase wit.

A good

A good man will love himſelf too well to loſe, and his neighbour alſo to win, an eſtate by gaming. Love of gaming corrupts the beſt principles in the world.

Gaming, like a quickſand, ſwallows up a man in a moment. Our follies and vices help one another, and blind the bubble, at the ſame time that they make the ſharper quickſighted.

Among many other evils that attend gaming, are theſe: *loſs of time*; *loſs of reputation*; *loſs of health*; *loſs of fortune*; *loſs of temper*; *ruin of families*; *defrauding of creditors*; *and what is often the effect of it, the loſs of life itſelf.*

Our pleaſures, for the moſt part, are ſhort, falſe, and deceitful; and, like drunkenneſs, revenge the jolly madneſs of *one* hour with the ſaid repentance of many.

Is there no better employment for people than luxury? What did they before they fell into theſe methods? Let pride pay, and exceſs be well excifed; and, if that will not cure, it will however help to keep the kingdom.

There is no remark more common among the ancient hiſtorians, than that, when the ſtate was corrupted with avarice and luxury, it was in danger of being betrayed or fold.

The inhabitants of the city of *Sybaris* were arrived to the height of luxury and voluptuoufnefs, that they taught their horfes to dance to the found of the flute; fo that the *Crotoniatæ*, who waged war with them, bringing a great number of pipers into the field of battle, fet their horfes a dancing, and fo broke their ranks; by which means they utterly overthrew them.

What is the difference, in effect, between old men and children, but that the one deals in paintings and ftatues, and the other in babies? So that we ourfelves are only the more expenfive fools.   *Sen.*

Pafcal kept always in mind this maxim, *avoid pleafure* and *fuperfluity.*

If they who affect an outward fhow, knew how many divide their trivial tafte, they would be afhamed of themfelves, and grow wifer, and beftow their fuperfluities in helping the needy, and befriending the neglected.   *Spec.*

Richnefs of drefs contributes nothing to a man of fenfe, but rather makes his fenfe in-

inquired into. The more the body is fet off, the mind appears the lefs.

Thofe men who deftroy a healthful conftitution of body by intemperance, and an irregular life, do as manifeftly kill themfelves, as thofe who hang, or poifon, or drown themfelves. *Sherlock.*

Recreations, moderately ufed, are profitable to the body for health, to the mind for refrefhment: but it is a note of a vain mind to be running after every garifh pomp or fhow.

The greateft pleafure wealth can afford us, is that of doing good. It is a happy thing, when a man's pleafure is alfo his perfection.

All men of eftates are, in effect, but truftees for the benefit of the diftreffed; and will be fo reckoned, when they are to give an account. *Bona.*

They that are lovers of pleafures, look upon all difcourfe of religion as canting. Eating and drinking, and vain mirth, news, and play, and the like, are their conftant entertainment; who know no other pleafures than what their five fenfes furnifh them with.

I   It

It is an infolence natural to the wealthy to affix, as much as in them lies, the character of a man to his circumftances. Take away, faid *Lactantius*, pride and boafting from rich men, and there will be no difference between a poor man and a rich.

A mean eftate is not to be contemned; nor the rich, that is foolifh, to be had in admiration.

In the flourifhing commonwealths of Greece and Rome, it was either fome brave action againft the enemy, or eminent juftice, virtue, or ability, that raifed one man above another; wealth had no fhare in it.

Caft an eye into the gay world, what fee we, for the moft part, but a fet of querulous, emaciated, fluttering, fantaftical beings, worn out in the keen purfuit of pleafure; creatures that know, own, condemn, deplore, yet ftill purfue their own infelicity? The decayed monuments of error! The thin remains of what is called delight! *Young.*

He only is worthy of efteem, that knows what is juft and honeft, and dares do it; that is mafter of his own paffions, and fcorns to be a flave to another's: fuch a one, in the loweft poverty, is a far better man, and merits more refpect, than thofe gay things,

who

who owe all their greatnefs and reputation to their rentals and revenues.

When we pity thofe that endure ficknefs and diftrefs, or any other temporal afflictions; let us remember, how much worfe it is with the profperous and gay finner; with them who are given over to a reprobate fenfe, and are cut off in the midft of their wickednefs.

We admire no man for enjoying all bodily pleafures to the full; this may create him envy, but not efteem. Whereas wifdom and prudence, true piety and virtue, and all the offices of humanity, charity, and friendfhip, have the praife and commendation, even of thofe who will not imitate them. The wife and good will be ever loved and honoured, as the glory of human nature. *Sherl.*

Of all the things this world affords us, the poffeffion and enjoyment of wifdom alone is immortal. A ftrict adherence to virtue, and a well-regulated life, renders our pleafures more folid and lafting.

If we apply ourfelves ferioufly to wifdom, we fhall never live without true pleafure, but learn to be pleafed with every thing. We fhall be pleafed fo far with

wealth,

wealth, as it makes us beneficial to others; with poverty, for not having much to care for; and with obfcurity, for being unenvied. *Plut.*

The *great* are under as much difficulty to expend with pleafure, as the *mean* to labour with fuccefs. *Young.*

There is a fweet pleafure in *contemplation*: all others grow flat and infipid upon frequent ufe; and when a man has run through a fet of vanities, in the declenfion of his age, he knows not what to do with himfelf if he cannot *think.*

Religion is fo far from barring men any innocent pleafure, or comfort of human life, that it purifies the pleafures of it, and renders them more grateful and generous; and, befide this, it brings mighty pleafures of its own, thofe of a glorious hope, a ferene mind, a calm and undifturbed confcience, which do far outrelifh the moft ftudied and artificial luxuries. *Sherl.*

There needs no train of fervants, no pomp or equipage, to make good our paffage to heaven; but the graces of a honeft mind will ferve us upon the way, and make us happy at our journey's end. *Sen.*

Of WOMEN, LOVE, and MARRIAGE.

THE utmost of a woman's character is contained in domestic life; first, her piety toward God, and, next, in the duties of a daughter, a wife, a mother, and a sister. *Spec.*

A prudent woman is in the same class of honour as a wise man. *Tat.*

Nothing can atone for the want of modesty and innocence; without which beauty is ungraceful, and quality contemptible. *Spec.*

The liberality of nature in the person is frequently attended with a deficiency in the understanding.

Women are always most observed, when they seem themselves least to observe, or to lay out for observation. *Johnson.*

Love cannot long be concealed, where it is; nor dissembled, where it is not. *Rochef.*

A good wife is a good portion: and there is nothing of so much worth as a mind well instructed.

Better is a portion *in* a wife, than *with* a wife.

Many

Many of the misfortunes in families arife from the trifling way women have in spending their time, and gratifying only their eyes and ears, inftead of their reafon and underftanding. *Tat.*

A lady who is tender of her reputation, would not be pleafed to hear herfelf applauded for her great fkill in finging and dancing. *Salluft,* fpeaking of *Sempronia,* a woman of great quality, but of a moft abandoned character, obferves, that fhe fung and danced with more art and grace, than became a virtuous woman.

There is nothing that wears out a fine face like the vigils of the card-table, and thofe cutting paffions which naturally attend them. Haggard looks, and pale complexions, are the natural indications of a female gamefter. *Addif.*

The plainer the drefs, with greater luftre does beauty appear. Virtue is the greateft ornament, and good fenfe the beft equipage. *Halifax.*

It requires but little acquaintance with the heart, to know that woman's firft wifh is to be handfome; and that confequently the readieft method of obtaining her kindnefs is to praife her beauty. *Johnfon.*

It

It is always to be underſtood, that a lady takes all you detract from the reſt of her ſex to be a gift to her. *Tat.*

A woman had need be perfectly provided of virtue, to repair the ruins of her beauty.

How vain are ſuch who are deſirous of life, yet would avoid old age: as if it were a reproach to look old! Tell a woman of her age, and perhaps you make her as deeply bluſh, as if you accuſed her of incontinency. *L'Eſtr.*

An inviolable fidelity, good humour, and complacency of temper, in a wife, outlive all the charms of a fine face, and make the decays of it inviſible. *Tat.*

Women can ſooner forgive great indiſcretions, than ſmall infidelities. *Rochef.*

It is ſeldom ſeen, that beautiful perſons are otherwiſe of great virtue. *Bacon.*

Howſoever a lewd woman may pleaſe a man for a time, he will hate her in the end, and ſhe will ſtudy to deſtroy him. *Raleigh.*

A woman of great ſpirit, and little underſtanding, expoſes herſelf to deriſion and reproach, and is deſpiſed wherever ſhe appears. *Tat.*

I 4 There

There are such perverse creatures, that fall to some men's lots, with whom it requires more than common proficiency in philosophy to be able to live. What charming companions for life are such women! *Spec.*

Alcibiades, being astonished at *Socrates'* patience, asked him, how he could endure the perpetual scolding of his wife: *Why*, said he, *as those do who are accustomed to the ordinary noise of wheels to draw water.*

He that contemns a shrew to the degree of not descending to word it with her, does worse than beat her. *L'Estr.*

A woman came to *Gratian*, the emperor, and with much clamour complained of her husband: to whom he mildly said, Woman, what are these things to me? Yes, said she; for he has also spoken many things against thy majesty: to which he replied, Woman, what is that to thee?

Solid love, whose root is virtue, can no more die, than virtue itself. *Eras.*

A courtesan taking notice to *Gelon*, king of Syracuse, that he had an ill breath; he asked his wife, why she did not tell him of it: I thought, said she, that all men's breath was alike.

Without

Without conftancy there is neither love, friendfhip, or virtue, in the world.

The reputation of a ftatefman, the credit of a merchant, and the modefty of a woman, prevail more than their power, riches, or beauty.

Sophocles, being afked, what harm he would wifh to his enemy; anfwered, that he might love where he was not liked.

As the poets reprefented the Graces under the figures of women; fo the Furies too. Let a woman be decked with all the embellifhments of art, and care of nature; yet, if boldnefs is to be read in her face, it blots all the lines of beauty.

There fcarce was ever any fuch thing under the fun, as an inconfolable widow. Grief is no incurable difeafe; but time, patience, and a little philofophy, with the help of human frailty and addrefs, will do the bufinefs. *L'Eftr.*

A woman bragging of her virtue looks as if it coft her fo much pains to get the better of herfelf, that the inferences are very ridiculous. *Halifax.*

Marriage has many pains, but celibacy has no pleafures. *Johnfon.*

I 5

The

The infelicities of marriage are not to be urged againſt its inſtitution, as the miſeries of life would prove equally, that life cannot be the gift of heaven. *Johnſon.*

Marriage is not commonly unhappy, but as life is unhappy; and moſt of thoſe who complain of connubial miſeries, have as much ſatisfaction as their natures would have admitted, or their conduct procured, in any other condition. *Johnſon.*

He who gets a good huſband for his daughter, has gained a ſon; and he who meets with a bad one, has loſt a daughter.

Marriage ſhould be conſidered as the moſt ſolemn league of perpetual friendſhip; a ſtate from which artifice and concealment are to be baniſhed for ever; and in which every act of diſſimulation is a breach of faith. *Johnſon.*

The emperor *Conrade*, when he beſieged *Guelpho*, duke of Bavaria, would not accept of any other conditions than that the men ſhould be priſoners; but that the women might go out of the town without violation of their honour, on foot, and with ſo much only as they could carry about them: which was no ſooner known, but they contrived preſently to carry out upon their ſhoulders
their

their hufbands and children, and even the duke himfelf. The emperor was fo affected with the generofity of the action, that he treated the duke and his people ever after with great humanity.

Themiftocles, being afked, how he would marry his daughter; whether to one of fmall fortune, but honeft; or to one that was rich, but of an ill reputation; *made anfwer*, I had rather have a man without an eftate, than have an eftate without a man.

When, after having dined too well, a hufband is received at home, without a ftorm, or a reproachful look, the wine will naturally work out all in kindnefs; which a wife fhould encourage, let it be wrapt up in ever fo much impertinence. *Halifax.*

When facrifices were offered to *Juno*, who prefided over marriage, the *gall* of the victim was thrown behind the altar, to fhow, that no fuch thing ought to be among married perfons.

Though *Solomon*'s defcription of a wife and good woman may be thought too mean and mechanical for this refined generation; yet certain it is, that the bufinefs of a family is the moft profitable and the moft

I 6   honorable

honorable study they can employ themselves in.

The surest way of governing, both a private family, and a kingdom, is for a husband, and a prince, to yield at certain times something of their prerogative.

Women should be acquainted, that no beauty has any charms, but the inward one of the mind; and that a gracefulness in their manners is much more engaging than that of their persons : that meekness and modesty are the true and lasting ornaments : for she that has these, is qualified as she ought to be for the management of a family, for the educating of children, for an affection to her husband, and submitting to a prudent way of living. These only are the charms that render wives amiable, and give them the best title to our respect. *Epict.*

Of TRUTH, LYING, and DISSIMULATION.

THERE is nothing fo delightful, fays *Plato*, as the hearing or the fpeaking of truth. For this reafon there is no converfation fo agreeable as that of the man of integrity, who hears without any defign to betray, and fpeaks without any intention to deceive.

Truth is always confiftent with itfelf, and needs nothing to help it out ; it is always near at hand, and fits upon our lips, and is ready to drop out before we are aware ; whereas a lie is troublefome, and fets a man's invention upon the rack ; and one trick needs a great many more to make it good. *Tillotf.*

Truth is the bafis of all excellence.

Tricks and treachery are the practice of fools, that have not fenfe enough to be honeft.

Plain truth muft have plain words; fhe is innocent, and accounts it no fhame to be feen naked: whereas the hypocrite or double-dealer fhelters and hides himfelf in ambiguities and referves. *Bona.*

Truth.

Truth has no gradations; nothing which admits of increafe can be fo much what it is as *truth is trnth*. There may be a *ftrange thing*, and a thing *more ftrange*. But if a propofition be *true*, there can be none *more true*. *Johnfon*.

Nothing appears fo low and mean, as lying and diffimulation; and it is obfervable, that only weak animals endeavour to fupply by craft the defects of ftrength, which nature has not given them.

Truth and falfehood, like the iron and clay in *Nebuchadnezzar*'s image, may cleave, but they will not incorporate. *Bacon*.

Truth may be expreffed without art or affectation: but a lie ftands in need of both.

Truth is born with us; and we muft do violence to nature, to fhake off our veracity. *St. Evr*.

A liar is a hector toward GOD, and a coward toward men.

There never was a hypocrite fo difguifed, but he had fome mark or other to be known by.

A honeft man is believed without an oath; for his reputation fwears for him.

Xenocrates

Xenocrates was a man of that truth and fidelity, that the *Athenians* gave him alone this privilege, *That his evidence should be lawful without swearing.* And it is said of *Fabricius*, that a man might as well attempt to turn the sun out of its course, as bring him to do a base or dishoneft action.

Truth is beft supported by virtue.

Such was the ingenuous simplicity of the primitive Chriftians; they looked upon it as a disparagement to be put to their oaths, thinking it sufficient for a good man to give this assurance of his truth, *I speak truly.* They counted it an impious thing even to dissemble the truth, and scorned to live upon such base terms to be beholden to hyprocrify for their lives.

It is common for men, governed by human reason, to invent various exceptions, to elude the force of verity. Nothing can be more defpicable and base, than for a man to speak contrary to his own knowledge and sense of things.

Truth in every thing is still the same, and, like its great Author, can be but one; and the fentence of reason ftands as firm as the foundation of the earth. Reafon is ever allied to truth.

When

When a man has forfeited the reputation of his integrity, he is set fast; and nothing will then serve his turn, neither truth nor falsehood. *Spec.*

Between falsehood and useless truth there is little difference. As gold, which he cannot spend, will make no man rich, so knowledge, which he cannot apply, will make no man wise. *Johnson.*

There are lying looks, as well as lying words; dissembling smiles, deceiving signs, and even a lying silence.

That kind of deceit which is cunningly laid, and smoothly carried on, under a disguise of friendship, is of all others the most impious and detestable.

Not to intend what you speak, is to give your heart the lie with your tongue: not to perform what you promise, is to give your tongue the lie with your actions.

A man who is rightly honest looks not to what he *might* do, but to what he *should:* he wears always the same countenance; speaks the truth; his cheeks are never stained with the blushes of recantation; nor does his tongue faulter to make good a lie with the secret glosses of a double or reserved meaning.

There

There is a kind of magic in truth, which forcibly carries the mind along with it. Men readily embrace the dictates of sincere reason.

Aristotle lays it down for a maxim, that *a brave man is clear in his discourse, and keeps close to truth.* And *Plutarch* calls lying, *the vice of a slave.*

There is no crime more infamous than the violation of truth; it is apparent, that men can be sociable beings no longer than they can believe each other. When speech is employed only as the vehicle of falsehood, every man must disunite himself from others, inhabit his one cave, and seek prey only for himself. *Johnson.*

Nothing can be more unjust or ungenerous, than to play upon the belief of a harmless person; to make him suffer for his good opinion, and fare the worse for thinking me a honest man.

It would be more obliging to say plainly, We cannot do what is desired; than to amuse people with fair words, that often put them upon false measures.

Great men must go and meet truth, if they are desirous to know it; for none will carry it to them.

There

There cannot be a greater treachery, than firſt to raiſe a confidence, and then deceive it. *Spec.*

Hypocritical piety is double iniquity.

There is no vice, that doth ſo cover a man with ſhame, as to be found falſe and perfidious. *Bacon.*

Truth alone, without eloquence, is ſufficiently powerful and perſuaſive; and ſtands in need of no ſtudied and artificial practices to vindicate and recommend it.

Sincerity is to ſpeak as we think; to do as we pretend and profeſs; to perform and make good what we promiſe; and really to be what we would ſeem and appear to be. *Tillotſ.*

A great man, on a certain affair, being aſked by *Heliogabalus*, how he durſt be ſo plain? Becauſe, *ſaid he*, I dare die: I can but die, if I ſpeak the truth; and I muſt die, if I flatter.

I had rather, ſaid *Lucian*, pleaſe by telling truth, than be diverting in telling tales; becauſe, if I be not agreeable, I may be uſeful.

The moſt deceitful are moſt ſuſpectful.

Deceit

Deceit and falfehood, whatever conveniencies they may for a time promife or produce, are in the fum of life obftacles to happinefs. Thofe who profit by the cheat diftruft the deceiver, and the act by which kindnefs was fought puts an end to confidence. *Johnfon.*

We muft not always fpeak all that we know; that were folly: but what a man fays fhould be what he thinks, otherwife it is knavery. All a man can get by lying and diffembling, is, that he fhall not be believed when he fpeaks truth. *Montaigne.*

A liar is fubject to two misfortunes; neither to believe, nor to be believed.

All the feeming family endearment, comfort, and complacency, which we figure to ourfelves at a diftance, what is it (too often!) but mutual attacks on the peace, plots on the riches, hopes from the ficknefs, and joy from the deaths, of each other? *Young.*

Did men take as much care to mend, as they do to conceal their failings, they would both fpare themfelves that trouble which diffimulation puts them to, and gain, over and above, the commendations they afpire to by their feeming virtues.

If

If faifehood, like truth, had but one face only, we fhould be upon better terms; for we fhould then take the contrary to what the liar fays, for certain truth. *Montaigne.*

Though many artifices may be ufed to maintain falfehood by fraud, they generally lofe their force by counteracting one another. *Johnfon.*

A hypocrite is under perpetual conftraint: and what a torment muft it be for a man always to appear different from what he really is! *Charron.*

Lying is a vice fo very infamous, that the greateft liars cannot bear it in other men.

Nothing is more noble, nothing more venerable, than fidelity. Faithfulnefs and truth are the moft facred excellencies and endowments of the human mind. *Cicero.*

Truth is fo great a perfection, fays *Pythagoras,* that if GOD would render himfelf vifible to men, he would choofe *light* for his *body,* and *truth* for his *foul.*

MIS-

MISCELLANIES.

NO one can be in a more unhappy cir-
cumftance, than to have neither an
ability to give or to take inftruction.

It is impoffible to make people underftand their *ignorance* ; for it requires knowledge to perceive it ; and therefore he that
can perceive it, has it not. *Taylor.*

There is a fort of economy in Providence
that one fhall excel, where another is defective, in order to make men more ufeful
to each other, and mix them in fociety.
Spec.

Knowledge is the treafure, but judgment
is the treafurer, of a wife man.

Where the fenfes, and their perceptions,
are vigoroufly employed, there the intellectual powers ceafe to act.

It is no diminution to have been in the
wrong. Perfection is not the attribute of
man. *Spec.*

The wife Heathens were glad to immor-
talize any one ferviceable gift, and overlook
all imperfections in the perfon who had it.
Tat.

A man's

A man's wisdom, economy, good sense, and skill in human life, if he be under misfortune, are of little use to him in the disposition of any thing. *Spec.*

It is observed in the course of worldly things, that men's fortunes are oftener made by their tongues, than by their virtues; and more men's fortunes overthrown thereby, than by their vices. *Raleigh.*

Though wit be lively and mantling, it is not often that it carries a great body with it.

Wit will never make a man rich, but there are places where riches will always make a wit. *Johnson.*

It is a noble science to know one's self well; and a noble courage to know how to yield.

There are four good mothers, of whom are often born four unhappy daughters: truth begets hatred; prosperity, pride; security, danger; and familiarity, contempt.

Some will read over, or rather over-read a book, with a view only to find fault: like venomous spiders, extracting a poisonous quality, where the industrious bees sip out a sweet and profitable juice.

Men

Men, like watches, are to be valued for their goings.

It is fufficient, that every one in this life do that well which belongs to his calling.

Frugality is good, if liberality be joined with it.

There is no wife and good man, that would change perfons and conditions intirely with any man in the world.

When a man draws himfelf into a narrow compafs, fortune has the leaft mark at him.

The wifeft of men have their follies, the beft have their failings, and the moft temperate have, now and then, their exceffes.

All ufelefs mifery is certainly folly, and he that feels evils before they come, may be defervedly cenfured; yet furely to dread the future, is more reafonable than to lament the paft. The bufinefs of life is to go forward; he who fees evils in profpect, meets it in his way; but he who catches it by retrofpection, turns back to find it. *Johnfcn.*

An univerfal applaufe is feldom lefs than two thirds of a fcandal. *L'Eftr.*

It

In this pleasant and jocular age, it is generally looked upon as a far more genteel and fashionable quality for a man to be witty, than wise.

The best way to secure observance is, not to insist too violently upon it.

None are so invincible as your half witted people; who know just enough to excite their pride, but not so much as to cure their ignorance.

One proffering to show *Themistocles* the art of memory, he answered, he had much rather he would teach him that of forgetfulness.

A man had better be poisoned in his blood, than in his principles.

There was a soldier that vaunted before *Julius Cesar* of the scars he had received on his face: *Cesar*, knowing him to be a coward, told him, You had best take heed next time you run away, how you look back.

Wise men mingle innocent mirth with their cares, as a help either to forget them, or overcome them: but to be *intemperate*, for the ease of one's mind, is to cure melancholy with madness.

It

It is in all things a profitable wifdom, to know when we have done enough.

Frugality is a fair fortune, and induftry a good eftate.

Some fee the errors and follies of mankind, and only make a jeft of them: they divert and entertain themfelves and others, by a comical reprefentation of a very tragical thing; as if no more were neceffary to teach men truth and virtue, than merely to expofe falfehood and vice.

Mutability is the badge of infirmity. It is feldom, that a man continues to wifh and defign the fame thing two days together. Now he is for marrying; and by and by a miftrefs is preferred before a wife: now he is ambitious and afpiring; prefently the meaneft fervant is not more humble than he: this hour he fquanders his money away; the next he turns mifer: fometimes he is frugal and ferious; at other times profufe, airy, and gay. *Charron.*

Ill qualities are catching, as well as difeafes; and the mind is at leaft as much, if not a great deal more, liable to infection, than the body.

There needs but one bad inclination to make a man vicious; but many good ones are neceffary to make him virtuous.

K   They

They who have a honest and engaging look, ought to suffer double punishment, if they belie it in their actions.

Every medal has its reverse. Every convenience carries its abatement.

Experience can never be infallible, because events are constantly unlike one another.

The soul is always busy; and if it be not exercised about serious affairs, will spend its activity upon trifles.

For a man to see and acknowledge his own ignorance and defects; to pretend to no more than he really has, and is; this single quality argues so much judgment, that there are few better testimonies to be given of it. *Char.*

By others faults, wise men correct their own.

It was said by *Diogenes*, that, to live well, one must oppose nature to law, reason to passion, and resolution to fortune.

He that makes others fear him, has reason to fear them.

Experience is the best adviser; but it is better to learn by others than our own.

3   We

We do not want precepts fo much as patterns, fays *Pliny*; and example is the fofteft and leaft invidious way of commanding.

Not to be addicted too much to any one thing, is the moft excellent rule of life.

Paft enjoyments do not alleviate prefent evils; whereas the evils a man has endured, heighten the prefent fatisfactions.

There are fewer higher gratifications than that of reflection on furmounted evils, when they were not incurred nor protracted by our fault, and neither reproach us with cowardice nor guilt. *Johnfon.*

Only that which is honeftly got, is gain.

It is a ftanding rule in philofophy, never to make the opinion of others the meafure of our behaviour.

Reafon is blinded by affection.

If you feem to approve of another man's wit, he will allow you to have judgment. *Guard.*

That which is known to three perfons, is no fecret.

No man has a thorough tafte of profperity, to whom adverfity never happened.

It

It was a noble faying of the *Lacedæmonians*, that they inquired not fo much *how many* their enemies were, but *where* they were.

King *John* was importuned by a courtier to unbury the bones of a perfon, who in his lifetime had been his great enemy: no, no, replied the king, I wifh all my enemies were as honorably buried.

One good head is better than a great many hands.

It is much greater kindnefs not to fuffer us to fall, than to lend a hand to lift us up. And a greater fatisfaction to be kindly received, and obtain nothing, than obtain what we defire, after having been expofed.

Requefts coft a reluctancy of nature, fearing to receive the difcourtefy of a denial. That which is beftowed too late, is next to not giving. *Gracian.*

Hope deferred makes the heart fick.

Pleafure nnd pain, though the moft unlike that can be, are yet fo contrived by nature, as to be conftant companions; and it is not amifs to obferve, that the fame motions and mufcles of the face are employed both in laughing and crying. *Char.*
Small

Small tranfgreffions become great by frequent repetition ; as fmall expences, mul-
tiplied, infenfibly wafte a large revenue.

When our vices leave us, we flatter ourfelves, that we leave them.

The remembrance of a crime committed
in vain, has been confidered as the moft
painful of all reflections. *Johnfon*.

At twenty years of age the will reigns ;
at thirty the wit ; and at forty the judgment. *Gracian*.

He is as great a fool that laughs at all
things, as he that frets at every thing.

There is nothing but is ominous to the
fuperftitious.

Voluntary rigour and torment is unnatural ; and it is as ridiculous to hate cheap
and eafy conveniencies, as it is mad and
foolifh to purchafe expenfive and uncom-
mon delicacies. *Char*.

All countries are a wife man's home.

Invention is the portion of ready wits,
and good choice that of folid judgment.

It is eafier to preferve health than to
recover it ; and to prevent difeafes, than to
cure them.

All

All objects lose by too familiar view. *Dryden.*

The best things, when corrupted, become the worst.

As no man lives so happy, but to some his life would seem unpleasant; so we find none so miserable, but one shall hear of another that would change calamities with him.

The more strength the body loses, the more the soul acquires.

Form is good, but no formality.

A talkative fellow, willing to learn of *Isocrates*, he asked him double his usual price; because, said he, I must both teach him to speak, and to hold his tongue.

We should choose to bear the hatred of evil men, rather than deserve their just accusation, after serving their base ends. *Plut.*

By the rules of justice, no man ought to to be ridiculed for any imperfection, who does not set up for eminent sufficiency in that way wherein he is defective.

To judge impartially, we are to put mens good qualities in the balance against their bad ones; and, if the scale of the first outweighs,

weighs, the latter ought not to be brought into account.

He that is fhamed to be feen in a mean condition, would be proud of a fplendid one. *Sen*.

If I had money, fays *Socrates*, I would buy me a cloak. They that knew he wanted one, fhould have prevented the very intimation of that want.

He that is little in his own eyes, will not be troubled to be thought fo in others.

Nothing violent is of long continuance. *Sen*.

It is commonly faid, that the jufteft dividend nature has given of her favours, is that of fenfe; for there is none that is not contented with his fhare.

It is as great a point of wifdom to hide ignorance, as to difcover knowledge.

Singularity, as it implies a contempt of general practice, is a kind of defiance, which juftly provokes the hoftility of ridicule. He therefore who indulges peculiar habits, is worfe than others, if he be not better. *Johnfon*.

No evil action can be well done; but a good one may be ill done.

To

To know how to forget is a happiness, rather than an art. Thoſe things are generally beſt remembered, which ought moſt to be forgot. Sometimes the remedy of an evil conſiſts in forgetting it; and that time it is we commonly forget the remedy.

Let a man do his beſt; and the world may do its worſt.

It was ſmartly ſaid by the *Egyptian*, who being aſked what it was he carried ſo cloſely; replied, *It was therefore covered, that it might be ſecret.*

Among the beſt of men there is hardly one to be found, but he is liable to be hanged ten times in his life, if all his actions and thoughts were ſtrictly to be examined. We are ſo far from being good, according to the laws of GOD, that we cannot be ſo according to our own.   *Mont.*

He that ſhoots at the ſtars, may hurt himſelf, but not endanger them.

It was bravely ſaid by *Antigonus*, who in a battle being told, that his enemies exceeded him in number; he aſked the reporter, againſt how many he reckoned *him?*

The moſt provident have commonly more to ſpare than men of great fortunes.

A mean

A mean freedom is more naturally defired than a golden fervitude. Fetters of gold are ftill fetters.

There is no courfe of life fo weak, as that which is carried on by exact rule and difcipline. The leaft debauch to fuch a man will ruin him. *Mont.*

An evennefs of living hath too much of confinement in it: men will be rather more or lefs, than always the fame.

Difficulty of atchievement ftupifies the fluggard, advifes the prudent, terrifies the fearful, animates the courageous.

Honefty is filently commended even by the practice of the moft wicked; for their deceit is under its colour.

It is not eafy to impofe the tongue's filence upon the heart's grievance.

He that will win the game, muft look more upon the mark than the money; if he hits the one he takes the other.

Thofe who are unwilling to do us any fervices, are never unprovided of excufes.

It is lefs difhonour to diflodge an army in the dark, than to be beaten in the light.

K 5   It

It is inhuman and arrogant to insult over a penitent delinquent.

In *Italy*, their ordinary form of asking is, *Do good for your own sake.*

A good cause makes a courageous heart. They that fear an overthrow, are half conquered.

The world can never be so bad, but a honest man will at one time or other be thought good for something.

As civil dissentions are the most unnatural, so nothing can appear more astonishing, than a war without an enemy.

He that scoffs at the crooked, had need go very upright himself.

Many a man would be extremely ridiculous, if he did not spoil the jest by playing upon himself first.

A tree that is every year transplanted, will never bear fruit ; and a mind that is always hurried from its proper station, will scarce ever do good in any.

The *Dutch* have a good proverb, *Thefts never enrich, alms never impoverish, prayers hinder no work.*

It

It is a known ftory of a friar, who on a faftingday bid his capon be carp, and then very canonically eat ir : by fuch a tranfubftantiating power, our wits bid all ferioufnefs and confideration be formality and foppery, and then under that name endeavour to drive it out of the world.

One may be a good advifer, though an ill folicitor.

There is as much difference between wit and wifdom, as between the talent of a buffoon and a ftatefman; and yet, in the ordinary courfe of the world, one paffes often for the other.

The pride of wit and knowledge is often mortified, by finding that they confer no fecurity againft the common errors which miflead the weakeft and meaneft of mankind. *Johnfon.*

Mercy to the evil proves cruelty to the innocent.

He that fhoots an arrow in jeft, may kill a man in earneft.

No men are fo often in the wrong, as thofe who pretend to be always in the right.

He gets a double victory, who overcomes himfelf, when he doth his enemy.

He

He has a good judgment, that relies not wholly on his own.

We can no more correct all ill opinions in the world, than heal all the diftempers that are in it.

There is as much wifdom in bearing with other people's defects, as in being fenfible of their good qualities; and we fhould make the follies of others rather a warning and inftruction to ourfelves, than a fubject of mirth and mockery of thofe that commit them. *Rochef.*

When we commend good and noble actions, we make them, in fome meafure, our own.

There are men of prey, as well as beafts of prey.

When a man owns himfelf to be in an error, he does but tell you in other words, that he is wifer than he was. *Swift.*

He that thinks of many things, thinks of nothing; and he that would go feveral ways, ftands ftill.

Forgetting of a wrong is a mild revenge.

It was a civil reprehenfion of a fidler to king *Philip*, who difputed with him about his playing: God forbid! faid he, that

your

your majefty fhould be fo unhappy as to underſtand a fiddle better than I do.

There is no contending with neceffity; and we fhould be very tender how we cenfure thofe that fubmit to it. It is one thing to be at liberty to do what we will, and another thing to be tied up to do what we muſt. *L'Eſtr.*

The only way to be happy and quiet is, to make all contingencies indifferent to us.

A divided family can no more ſtand, than a divided commonwealth.

They who live under a tyranny, and have learned to admire its power as facred and divine, are debauched as much in their religion, as in their morals. *Shaftſb.*

There are none that fall fo unpitied, as thofe that have raifed themfelves upon the fpoils of the public.

One general mark of an impoftor is, that he outdoes the original.

It is good to rectify our natures, but not to force them.

Men can better fuffer to be denied, than to be deceived.

The gifts of the mind are able to cover the defects of the body; but the perfections

of

of the body cannot hide the imperfections of the mind.

They that feed on wisdom, shall yet be hungry, and they that drink her, shall yet be thirsty.

A man that doth the best he can, doth all that he should do.

In nature nothing is superfluous. *Arist*.

Fortune is never more deceitful, than when she seems most to favour. He that is rich to-day may be poor to-morrow.

As dreams are the fancies of those that sleep, so fancies are but the dreams of men awake.

The strongest heads are commonly the weakest.

A habit of secrecy is both politic and moral.

Counsel and wisdom atchieve more and greater exploits than force.

Cato observed, that wise men learn more by fools, than fools by wise men: for they see their weakness, to avoid it; these consider not their virtues to imitate them.

A person

A perfon being afked, how old he was, anfwered, I am in health: being afked, how rich he was, he faid, I am not in debt.

The pity of tears only, is too waterifh to do good.

Nothing promotes fixation of thought more than the clofing of our eyes; for according to the Arabian proverb, when the five windows, thofe of the fenfe, are fhut up, the houfe of the mind is then fulleft of light.

That is done foon enough, which is done well enough.

It is the intention, morally fpeaking, that makes the action good or bad; and even brutes themfelves will put a difference between harms of illwill and mifchance.

He that follows nature is never out of his way. Nature is fometimes fubdued, but feldom extinguifhed. *Bacon.*

To be eminent in a low profeffion is to be great in little, and fomething in nothing.

We read of an aftrologer, that foretold his own end to the very day and hour: He lived perfectly in health till the laft
minute

minute of his time, and then hanged himfelf for the honour of his prediction.

Money makes not fo many true friends,
as it makes enemies.

Man, at the beft, is but a compofition
of good and evil. Diamonds have flaws,
and rofes have prickles: the fun has its
fhade, and the moon its fpots.

Civility is a kind of charm that attracts
the love of all men; and too much is better than to fhow too little.

He that contends with natural averfions,
doth the fame thing as if he undertook to
cure incurable difeafes.

It is not fo painful to a honeft man to
want money, as it is to owe it.

He has made a good progrefs in bufinefs, that has thought well of it beforehand.
Some *do* firft, and *think* afterward.

It is better to fuffer without a caufe, than
that there fhall be a caufe for our fuffer-
ing.

The lefs wit a man has, the lefs he knows
that he wants it.

A heart without fecrecy is an open letter for every one to read.

Thofe

Thofe beft can bear reproof, who merit praife.

The itch of knowing fecrets is naturally accompanied with another itch of telling them.

To tell our own fecrets is generally folly, but that folly is without guilt. To communicate thofe with which we are entrufted, is always treachery, and treachery for the moft part combined with folly. *Johnfon*.

In all fortunes and extremes, a great foul will never want matter to work upon. There is no condition, but what fits well upon a wife man.

He that hinders not a mifchief, when it is in his power, is guilty of it.

There is no rule that is not liable to fome exception or other, faving that very rule itfelf.

He that has feweft faults, has conftructively none at all, becaufe it is a common cafe: but no man has more faults, than he that pretends to have none.

We may hate mens vices, without any illwill to their perfons; but we cannot help

help defpifing thofe that have no kind of virtue to recommend them.

Precipitation ruins the beft-laid defigns; whereras patience ripens the moft difficult, and renders the execution of them eafy.

Doing juftice to worthy qualities, is a credit to our judgment.

A fprightly generous *horfe* is able to carry a packfaddle as well as an *afs*; but he is too good to be put to the drudgery. *Swift*.

Though an action be ever fo glorious in itfelf, it ought not to pafs for great, if it be not the effect of wifdom and good defign.

When two perfons compliment one another with the choice of any thing, each of them generally gets that which he likes leaft. *Swift*.

It was a maxim with *Cefar*, that we ought to reckon we have done nothing, fo long as any thing remains to be done.

What is *rational* carries its own weight.

Too auftere a philofophy makes few wife men; too rigorous politics, few good fub-jects;

jects; too hard a religion, few religious perfons, whofe devotion is of long continuance. *St. Evr.*

It is in vain to charm the ears, or gratify the ears, if the mind be not fatisfied.

To be a *cynic* is as bad as to be a *fycophant*.

He that writes an infipid panegyric upon another, libels himfelf. *Voiture.*

How different foever mens fortunes may be, there is always fomething or other that balances the ill and the good, and makes all even at laft.

He that would be fure to have his bufinefs well done, muft either do it himfelf, or fee the doing of it.

A great part of mankind employ their firft years to make their laft miferable.

It is eafier to avoid a fault, than to acquire a perfection.

Men of indifferent parts are apt to condemn every thing above their own capacity. He muft be a very unfit judge of wit, who innocently believes, that he has himfelf as much as any man needs to have.

The fame rule, that *a difeafe well known is half cured,* holds as true in the diftempers

of

of the mind, as in the indifpofitions of the body.

It is difficult for a man to have fenfe, and be a knave. A true and folid genius conducts to order, truth, and virtue.

A great many people are fond of books, as they are of furniture; to drefs and fet off their rooms, more than to adorn and enrich their minds.

If a man cannot find eafe within himfelf, it is to little purpofe to feek it any-where elfe.

Thofe are prefumed to be the beft coun-fels, which come from them that advife againft their own intereft.

One month in the fchool of affliction will teach us more wifdom, than the grave precepts of *Ariftotle* in feven years.

Remove the caufe, and the effect will ceafe.

Gentlenefs is the beft way to make a man loved and refpected in his family: he makes himfelf contemptible, when he talks paffionately to his fervants, for no reafon but to fhow his authority.

It is dangerous to attack a man you have deprived of means to efcape.

There

There is nothing more to be wondered at, than that men who have lived long ſhould wonder at any thing.

None but thoſe we are nearly concerned for, or are to anſwer for, ſhould make us ſolicitous about their conduct. The way to live eaſy is to mind our own buſineſs, and leave others to take care of theirs.

Men may give good advice; but they cannot give the ſenſe to make a right uſe of it.

Advice, like phyſic, ſhould be ſo ſweetened and prepared, as to be made palatable; or nature may be apt to revolt againſt it.

When there are ſo many thouſands of dangers hovering about us, what wonder is it, if one comes to hit at laſt?

A man is ſeldom ſucceſsful, that is diffident of himſelf.

All fools are not knaves; but all knaves are fools.

It goes a great way toward making a man faithful, to let him underſtand, that you think him ſo; and he that does but ſuſpect that I will deceive him, gives me a kind of right to cozen him.

Thoſe

Thofe who believe all the good fpoken of themfelves, and all the evil fpoken of others, are unhappily miftaken on both fides.

Reading ferves for delight, for ornament, and for ability; it perfects nature, and is perfected by experience.

There is certainly no greater happinefs than to be able to look back on a life ufe-fully and virtuoufly employed; to trace our own progrefs in exiftence, by fuch tokens as excite neither fhame nor forrow. It ought therefore to be the care of thofe who wifh to pafs the laft hours with comfort, to lay up fuch a treafure of pleafing ideas, as fhall fupport the expences of that time, which is to depend wholly upon the fund already acquired. *Johnfon.*

COUN-

C O U N S E L S.

THERE feems, fays *Seneca*, to be fo near an affinity between wifdom, philofophy, and good counfels, that it is rather matter of curiofity, than of profit to divide them.

Good counfel is caft away upon the arrogant, the felf-conceited, and the ftupid; who are either too proud to take it, or too heavy to underftand it.

Plato often inculcates this great precept, *Do thine own work, and know thyfelf.*

If thou wilt be happy, correct thy imagination by reafon; reject opinion, and live according to nature.

Let reafon go before every enterprife, and counfel before every action.

Be not diverted from your duty by any idle reflections the filly world may make upon you; for their cenfures are not in your power, and confequently fhould not be any part of your concern. *Epict.*

Sell not virtue to purchafe wealth.

Reft fatisfied with doing well, and leave others to talk of what they pleafe.

Pitch

Pitch upon that courſe of life which is the moſt excellent; and cuſtom will render it the moſt delightful. *Pythag.*

Rather avoid thoſe vices you are naturally inclined to, than aim at thoſe excellencies and perfections which you were never made for. *Cicero.*

Live in peace with all men; nevertheleſs have but one counſellor of a thouſand.

Never defer that till to-morrow, which you can do to-day. Never do that by proxy, which you can do yourſelf.

Deliberate long of what you can do but once.

When the idea of any pleaſure ſtrikes your imagination, make a juſt computation between the duration of the pleaſure, and that of the repentance ſure to follow it. *Epiſt.*

Be always at leiſure to do good; never make buſineſs an excuſe to decline the offices of humanity. *Antoninus.*

Do good with what thou haſt, or it will do thee *no* good.

Avoid all ſourneſs and auſterity of manners. Virtue is a pleaſant and agreeable quality;

quality; and gay and civil wisdom is always engaging.

Forget the faults of others, and remember thine own.

Whatever you dislike in another person, take care to correct in yourself, by the gentle reproof of a better practice. *Sprat.*

Hear not ill of a friend, nor speak any of an enemy. Believe not all your hear, nor report all you believe.

Approve yourself to wise men by your virtue, and take all the rest by your civilities.

Avoid popularity: it has many snares, but no real benefit.

Imprint this maxim deeply in your mind, that there is nothing certain in this human and mortal state; by which means you will avoid being transported with prosperity, and being dejected in adversity.

Do nothing to-day, that you will repent of to-morrow.

Seek not out the things that are too hard for you. Strive not in a matter that concerns you not.

If your means suit not with your ends, pursue those ends which suit with your means.

L   Be

Be rather bountiful than expensive : neither make nor go to feasts.

Rise from table with an appetite, and you will never sit down without one.

Make yourself agreeable as much as possible to all; for there is no person so contemptible, but that it may be in his power to be your best friend, or worst enemy.

Defer not charities till death; he that doth so, is rather liberal of another man's, than of his own.   *Bacon.*

Reckon upon benefits well placed, as a treasure that is laid up; and account thyself the richer for that which thou givest a worthy person.

In the morning, think what thou hast to do; and at night, ask thyself what thou hast done.

Have a care of vulgar errors : dislike, as well as allow, reasonably : follow the dictates of your reason, and you are safe.

Learn the art of entertaining thyself alone, without being weary or melancholy; and then thou wilt not be much put to it for want of recreation and company.

Account it no disgrace to be censured of those men, whose favours would be no credit

credit to thee. Thou thyfelf only knoweft what thou art; others only guefs at thee: rely not therefore on their opinions; but ftick to thine own confcience.

In all the affairs of human life, let it be your care, not to hurt your mind, nor offend your judgment. *Epict.*

Do no fecret thing before a ftranger; for you know not what he will bring forth.

Think before you fpeak, and confider before you promife. Take time to deliberate and advife; but loofe no time in executing your refolutions.

Let not your zeal for a caufe pufh you into a hazardous engagement. Set bounds to your zeal by difcretion, to error by truth, to paffion by reafon, to divifions by charity.

Spend the day well, and you will rejoice at night.

Never expect any affiftance or confolation in your neceffities from drinking companions.

Do well, and fear neither man nor devil. Keep good company, and the devil will not dare to make one.

Medi-

Meditate often upon eternity, and no accidents of this mortal life will trouble you.

Always take part with and defend the unfortunate.

Strive not with a man without caufe. Blame not before thou haft examined the truth. Debate thy caufe with thy neighbour himfelf, and difcover not a fecret to another.

Never reveal thy fecrets to any, except it is as much their intereft to keep them, as it is thine they fhould be kept. Only truft thyfelf, and another fhall not betray thee.

Endeavour to make peace among thy neighbours: it is a worthy and reputable action, and will bring greater and jufter commendations to thee, and more benefit to thofe with whom thou converfeft, than wit or learning, or any of thofe fo much admired accomplifhments. *Fuller*.

Take heed of whom you fpeak, and to whom.

Have not to do with any man in his paffion; for men are not, like iron, to be wrought upon when they are hot.

Purfue not a coward too far, left you make him turn valiant to your difadvantage.

Speak

Speak not in the ears of a fool; for he will defpife the wifdom of your words. Caft not your pearls before fwine.

If you be confulted concerning a perfon, either very inconftant, paffionate, or vicious, give not your advice; it is in vain: for fuch will do only what fhall pleafe themfelves.

Avoid, as much as you can, the company of all vicious perfons whatfoever; for no vice is alone, and all are infectious.

Whenever you difcourfe, confine yourfelf to fuch fubjects as are neceffary, and exprefs your fenfe in as few words as you can. *Epict.*

Be not eafily exceptious, nor rudely familiar; the one will breed contention, the other contempt.

If a thing be not fitting, do it not: if it be not true, fpeak it not. *Antoninus.*

Take not pleafure in much good cheer, neither be tied to the expence thereof. Banquet not upon borrowing. If thou be the mafter of a feaft, lift not thyfelf up; but be among them as one of the reft.

Ufe temporal things, but defire eternal.

L 3 Pre-

Prefer folid fenfe to wit; never ftudy to be diverting without being ufeful; let no jeft intrude upon good manners; nor fay any thing that may offend modefty.

Take care of a reconciled enemy, and an untried friend.

Never triumph over any man's imperfection; but confider if the party, taxed for his deficiency in fome things, may not likewife be praifed for his proficiency in others.

Be not hafty in your tongue, and in your deeds flack and remifs. Let not your hand be ftretched out to receive, and fhut when you fhould repay.

In converfation condefcend to compliance, rather than continue a difpute.

Speak with the vulgar, but think with the wife.

Let him that knows but little in his profeffion, keep to what he knows beft; for, if he be not reckoned dextrous at it, he will at leaft be counted folid. *Gracian.*

Never antedate your own misfortunes; for many times men make themfelves more miferable than indeed they are; and the apprehenfion of infelicity doth more afflict them than the infelicity itfelf.

In

In marriage, prefer the perſon before wealth, virtue before beauty, and the mind before the body; then you have a wife, a friend, and a companion.

Obey the magiſtrate, and the law, but not ſervilely: obſerve ceremonies, but not ſuperſtitiouſly.

He who will take no advice, but be always his own counſellor, ſhall be ſure to have a fool for his client.

Boaſt not of thy good deeds, left thy evil deeds be alſo laid to thy charge.

In all differences, conſider that both you and your enemy are dropping off; and that ere long your very memories will be extinguiſhed.. *Antoninus.*

Give not over thy mind to heavineſs: the gladneſs of the heart is the life of man; and the joyfulneſs of a man prolongeth his days. Remove ſorrow far from thee; for ſorrow has killed many, and there is no profit therein; and carefulneſs bringeth age before the time.

To be free minded and cheerfully diſpoſed at the hours of meat, and of ſleep, is one of the beſt precepts for long life. *Bacon.*

Be

Be flow·in choofing a friend, and flower to change him; courteous to all; intimate with few; flight no man for his meannefs, nor efteem any for their wealth and greatnefs.

Infult not over mifery, nor deride infirmity. The frogs in the well faid pertinently to the boys that pelted them, *Children, though this be fport to you, it is death to us.*

Blemifh not thy good deeds, neither ufe uncomfortable words, when thou giveft any thing; but in all thy gifts fhow a cheerful countenance.

In all matters of religion, let your duty be the motive. In all things of common life, let reafon direct you. *Sherlock.*

Whether young or old, think it not too foon, or too late, to turn over the leaves of your paft life; and confider what you would do, if what you have done were to do again.

They were three good leffons which the bird in the fable gave the fowler for his releafe. Not to lofe a certainty for an uncertainty: not to give credit to things beyond probability: not to grieve for that which is paft remedy.

Boaft

Boaſt not of thyſelf, for it ſhall bring contempt upon thee; neither deride another, for it is dangerous.

From the experience of others, do thou learn wiſdom; and from their failings, correct thine own faults.

Refuſe the favours of a mercenary man, they will be a ſnare unto thee, and thou ſhalt never be quit of the obligation.

Uſe not to-day, what to-morrow may want; neither leave that to hazard, which foreſight may provide for, or care prevent.

Work while it is called to-day, for you know not how much you may be hindered to-morrow. One to-day is worth two to-morrows. *Franklin.*

At every action and enterpriſe, aſk yourſelf this queſtion, What will the conſequence of this be to me? Am I not likely to repent of it? I ſhall be dead in a little time, and then all is over with me. *Antoninus.*

Whatſoever you take in hand, remember the end, and you ſhall never do amiſs.

L 5 Or

Of TIME, BUSINESS, and RECREATION.

THE ordinary manner of spending their time, is the only way of judging of any one's inclination and genius.

No man can be provident of his time, that is not prudent in the choice of his company.

The advantage of living does not confift in length of days, but in the right improvement of them. As many days as we pafs without doing fome good, are fo many days intirely loft. *Montaigne.*

We fhould read over our lives, as well as books; take a furvey of our actions, and make an infpection into the divifion of our time. King *Alfred* is recorded to have divided the day and night into three parts; eight hours he allotted to eat and fleep in; eight for bufinefs and recreation; and eight he dedicated to ftudy and prayer.

Some people are bufy, and yet do nothing; they fatigue and weary themfelves out; and yet drive at no point, nor propofe any general end of action or defign. *Antoninus.*

To

To come but once into the world, and trifle away our right ufe of it, making that a burden, which was given for a blefling, is ftrange infatuation.

There is but little need to drive away that time by foolifh divertifements, which flies away fo fwiftly of itfelf; and, when once gone, is never to be recalled.

He is idle, that might be better employed. The idle man is more perplexed what to do, than the induftrious in doing what he ought.

There is nothing that fo much engages our affections to this world, as the want of confideration, how foon we are to leave it.

This day is only ours; we are dead to yefterday, and we are not yet born to the morrow.

Time is what we want moft, but what we ufe worft; for which we muft all account, when time fhall be no more.

A wife man counts his minutes, he lets no time flip; for time is life; which he makes long, by the good hufbandry of a right ufe and application of it.

There are but very few who know how to be idle and innocent. By doing nothing, we learn to do ill. *Spec.*

L 6   An

An idle boy is a kind of monster in the creation: all nature is busy about him. How wretched is it to hear people complain, that the day hangs heavy upon them; that they do not know what to do with themselves! How monstrous are such expressions among creatures, who can apply themselves to the duties of religion and meditation; to the reading of useful books: who may exercise themselves in the pursuits of knowledge and virtue, and every hour of their lives make themselves wiser and better than they were before! *Addif.*

Make the most of your minute (says the emperor *Antoninus*) and be good for something, while it is in your power.

Time ought, above all other kinds of property, to be free from invasion; and yet there is no man who does not claim the power of wasting that time which is the right of others. *Johnson.*

This is the supreme point of wisdom: to do only such things at the time when we are in the greatest probability of living, which we would do, if we were in the present expectance of dying.

How unreasonable is it to begin to live, when we can live no longer! That man does

does not live as he fhould do, who does not reckon upon every day as his laft.

Moft men that affect fports, make them a principal part of their life; not reflecting, that, while they are diverting the time, they are throwing it away. We alter the very nature and defign of recreation, when we make a bufinefs of it.

Of all the diverfions of life, there is none fo proper to fill up its empty fpaces, as the reading of ufeful and entertaining authors; and, with that, the converfation of a well chofen friend. *Spec.*

A man of letters never knows the plague of idlenefs: when the company of his friends fail him, he finds a remedy in reading, or in compofition. *St. Evr.*

He that is well employed in his ftudy, though he may feem to do nothing, does the greateft things yet of all others: he lays down precepts for the governing of our lives, and the moderating of our paffions; and obliges human nature, not only in the prefent, but in all fucceeding generations. *Sen.*

A wife man will difpofe of time paft to obfervation and reflection; time prefent, to duty; and time to come, to Providence.
Epami-

Epaminondas, prince of Thebes, had such hatred to idleness, that, finding one of his captains asleep in the daytime, he slew him; for which act being reproved by his nobles, he replied, *I left him as I found him*; comparing idle men to dead men.

The ruins of time are the monuments of morality.

He that follows his recreation instead of his business, shall in a little time have no business to follow.

Whosoever is engaged in a multiplicity of business, must transact much by substitution, and leave something to hazard; and he that attempts to do all, will waste his life in doing little.   *Johnson*.

None but a wise man can employ leisure well; and he that makes the best use of his time, has none to spare.

Employ your time well, if you mean to gain leisure; and, since you are not sure of a minute, throw not away an hour.

Leisure is time for doing something useful; this leisure the diligent man will obtain, but the lazy man never; for a life of leisure, and a life of laziness, are two things. *Franklin*.

Want

Want is little to be dreaded, when a man has but a short time left to be miserable.

Of all poverty, that of the mind is most deplorable.

All who exceed the age of sixty, except the latter part of it is spent in the exercise of virtue, and contemplation of futurity, must necessarily fall into an indecent old age. An inquisitive and virtuous soul improves daily in knowledge; and though the body decays, and all bodily pleasures with it; wisdom and counsel, piety and devotion, is the crown and glory of age.

If age puts an end to our desires of pleasure, and does the business of virtue, there can be no cause of complaint.

Things past, present, and to come, are strangely uniform, and of a colour; so that upon the matter, forty years of human life may serve for a sample of ten thousand.

If time be of all things the most precious, wasting time must be the greatest prodigality, since lost time is never found again, and what we call time enough, always proves little enough. *Franklin.*

Should the greatest part of people sit down, and draw up a particular account of their time, what a shameful bill would it be !

be ! So much extraordinay for eating, drinking, and sleeping, beyond what nature requires; so much in revelling and wantonness; so much for the recovery of the last night's intemperance; so much in gaming, plays, and masquerades; so much in paying and receiving formal and impertinent visits, in idle and foolish prating, in censuring and reviling our neighbours; so much in dressing our bodies, and talking of fashions; and so much wasted and lost in doing nothing. *Sherlock.*

It was a memorable practice of *Vespasian*, throughout the whole course of his life : he called himself to an account every night for the actions of the past day; and as often as he found he had slipt any one day without doing some good, he entered upon his diary this memorial, *I have lost a day.*

The greatest loss of time is delay and expectation, which depends upon the future. We let go the present, which we have in our power, and look forward to that which depends upon chance, and so quit a certainty for an uncertainty. *Seneca.*

The inconstancy of man's nature, and the mutability of things, occasion endless revolutions: we either improve or grow worse continually.

It

It is with our time, as with our eftates; a good hufband makes a little go a great way.

Some men are exceeding diligent in acquiring a vaft compafs of learning; fome in afpiring to honours and preferments; fome in heaping up riches; others are intent upon pleafures and diverfions; hunting, or play, vain contrivances, to pafs away their time: others are taken up in ufelefs fpeculations; others fet up for men of bufinefs, and fpend all their days in hurry and noife: but amid this variety, few apply themfelves to the wifdom, which fhould direct their lives. *Char*.

It is the great art and philofophy of life to make the beft of the prefent, whether it be good, or bad; and to bear the one with refignation and patience, and enjoy the other with thankfulnefs and moderation.

We muft be bufy about good, or evil; and he to whom the *prefent* offers nothing, will often be looking backward on the *paft*. *Johnfon*.

The time prefent is the only time we have to repent in, to ferve God, to do good to men, to improve our knowledge,

to

to exercife our graces, and to prepare for a bleffed immortality. *Sherlock.*

Within a while the earth fhall cover us all ; and then fhe herfelf fhall have her change. Now any man that fhall confider this, can he otherwife but contemn, in his heart, and defpife all worldly things? *Antoninus.*

There is no man but has a foul ; and, if he will look carefully to that, he need not complain for want of bufinefs. Where there are fo many corruptions to mortify, fo many inclinations to watch over, fo many temptations to refift, the graces of God to improve, and former neglects of all thofe to lament, fure there can never want fuffi-cient employment; for all thefe require time : and fo men at their deaths find; for thofe who have lived carelefly, and wafted their time, would then give all the world to redeem it.

OF

Of RETIREMENT, and the PRIVATE LIFE.

IT is an extraordinary attainment, and shows a well-composed mind, when a man loves to keep company with himself; and a virtue, as well as advantage, to take satisfaction and content in that enjoyment. *Char*.

Solitude can be well fitted, and set right but upon very few persons: they must have knowledge enough of the world, to see the follies of it; and virtue enough to despise all vanity. *Cowley*.

He that has renounced external things, and withdrawn into himself, is invincible: the world to him is as a prison, and solitude a paradise. *Bona*.

There is a vast difference between the *dull* person that is really so, and the *thinking* person that seems so: though both are not good company for others, yet the latter is excellent company to himself.

The more a man is contemplative, the more happy he is, and assimilated to the divine essence. *Aristotle*.

Solitude

Solitude relieves us, when we are fick of company; and converfation, when we are weary of being alone.

As too long a retirement weakens the mind, fo too much company diffipates it.

By *reading* we enjoy the dead, by *converfation*, the living, and by *contemplation*, ourfelves: reading enriches the memory, converfation polifhes the wit, and contemplation improves the judgment: of thefe, reading is the moft important, as it furnifhes both the others.

A man may be a firft rate in virtue and true value, and yet be very obfcure as to the world at the fame time. *Antoninus.*

Self-fufficiency and felf-fatisfaction are but other words for happinefs; and thefe are never to be had, but by learning to entertain ourfelves well with our own thoughts. *Char.*

Antifthenes, the philofopher, being afked, What fruit he gained by his ftudies; anfwered, He had learned to live and converfe with himfelf.

The filent virtues of a good man in folitude are more amiable than all the noify honours of active life. *Pope.*

That

That calm and elegant satisfaction, which the vulgar call melancholy, is the true and proper delight of men of knowledge and virtue. What we take for diversion is but a mean way of entertainment in comparison of that which is considering and knowing ourselves. *Tat.*

It is the character of a consummate merit to be able to live in a retreat with honour, after one has lived in public with splendor. *St. Evr.*

There is a time when the claims of the public are satisfied; then a man might properly retire to review his life, and purify his heart.

Charles V, emperor of Germany, resigned all his dominions, and retired to a monastery; had his own funeral celebrated before his face; and left this testimony of the Christain religion, *That the sincere profession of it, had in it sweets and joys that courts were strangres to.*

Sir *Francis Walsingham,* toward the end of his life, grew very melancholy, and writ to lord *Burleigh* to this purpose: We have lived long enough to our country, to our fortunes, and to our sovereign: it is high time we begin to live to ourselves, and to our GOD.

Sir

Sir *Henry Wotton*, who had gone on several embaffies, and was intimate with the greateft princes, chofe to retire from all; faying, The utmoft happinefs a man could attain to, was to be at leifure to *be*, and to *do* good. When reflecting on his former years, he would fay, How *much* time have I to repent of! and how *little* to do it in.

Some fufpenfion of common affairs, fome paufe of temporal pain and pleafure, is doubtlefs neceffary to him that deliberates for eternity, who is forming the only plan in which mifcarriage cannot be repaired, and examining the only queftion in which miftake cannot be rectified. *Johnfon*.

He who refigns the world, is in conftant poffeffion of a ferene mind; but he who follows the pleafures of it, meets with nothing but remorfe and confufion. *Spec*.

The *country* is the place from whence the *court*, as in its true diftance, appears full of charms, and worthy our admiration: but, if a man come near it, its perfections decreafe, juft as thofe of a fine landfkip, when you behold it at a clofe view.

Princes and their grandees, of all men are the unhappieft; for they live leaft alone.

A firft

A firſt miniſter of ſtate has not ſo much buſineſs in public, as a wiſe man has in private. *Cowley.*

A ſolitary life has no charms for an ambitious mind. *Fenelon.*

In ſolitude, if we eſcape the example of bad men, we likewiſe want the counſel and converſation of the good. *Johnſon.*

True happineſs is of a retired nature, and an enemy to pomp and noiſe : it ariſes, in the firſt place, from the enjoyment of one's ſelf ; and, in the next, from the friendſhip and converſation of a few ſelect companions.

The man that lives retired, lives quiet ; he fears nobody, of whom nobody is afraid. He that ſtands below on the firm ground, need not fear falling.

To live at a diſtance from, yet near enough to do good to men, is acting like a benign deity on earth. *Fenelon.*

It was an excellent ſaying of the elder *Scipio Africanus :* He never was leſs alone than when alone.

A wiſe man, that lives up to the principles of reaſon and virtue, if one conſider him in his ſolitude, as taking in the ſyſtem
of

of the univerſe, obſerving the mutual
dependence and harmony, by which the
whole frame of it hangs together, raiſing
his thoughts with magnificent ideas of Providence ; makes a nobler figure in the eye
of an intelligent being, than the greateſt
conqueror amid all the pomps and ſolem-
nities of a triumph.   *Tat.*

Though the continued traverſes of fortune may make us out of humour with the
world ; yet nothing but a noble inclination
to virtue and philoſophy can make us happy in retirement.

The pleaſure which affects a human mind
with the moſt lively and tranſporting touch-
es, is the ſenſe that we act in the eye of infinite wiſdom, power, and goodneſs, that
will crown our virtuous endeavours here,
with a happineſs hereafter, large as our deſires, and laſting as our immortal ſouls :
without this the higheſt ſtate of life is in-
ſipid, and with it the loweſt is a paradiſe.
Addiſ.

OF

OF SCEPTICISM AND INFIDELITY.

IT was a saying among the ancients, That even *Jupiter* could not please all. But we find now, that the true God himself is not free from the imputation of his audacious creatures, who impiously presume to quarrel with his revelation, as well as his providence; and express no more reverence to what he has dictated, than to what he doth. *Boyle.*

We are falling into an age of vain philosophy (as the apostle calls it) and so desperately overrun with drolls and sceptics, that there is hardly any thing so certain and so sacred, that is not exposed to question or contempt. *L'Estr.*

God has expresly declared, that death shall open a passage to a blessed eternity; and yet some have doubts and diffidence about it. What is this, but to be a stranger to the divine attributes, and distrust the promises of our Saviour; to fail in the main requisites of a christian, and turn infidel in a society of believers? *Col.*

Our present sticklers for atheism consist chiefly of such who never troubled them-

M   selves

felves fo much as to underftand the firft
principles of religion: their ftudy has been
employed another way, *viz.* in courtly
forms of fpeech, and punctilios of action;
in fafhionable garbs, and artificial luxuries;
but, as, for the feverer and more ufeful
ftudies, they bequeath them to the dull men
of fenfe and reafon.   *Scott.*

I can hardly think that man to be in his
right mind, fays *Cicero,* who is deftitute of
religion.

An atheift is the moft vain pretender to
reafon in the world.   The whole ftrength
of atheifm confifts in contradicting the univerfal reafon of mankind.   They have no
principles, nor can have any; and therefore
they can never reafon, but only confidently
deny and affirm.   *Sherlock.*

Practical atheifm has always been the
grand fupport of fpeculative; and defervedly efteemed no lefs dangerous in its ten-
dency and effects.

Nothing can be plainer, than that ignorance and vice are two ingredients abfolutely neceffary in the compofition of free-
thinkers, who, in propriety of fpeech, are
no thinkers at all.   *Swift.*

2   They

They lie, says *Seneca*, who say they believe there is no God: though they may profess this somewhat confidently in the day-time, when they are in company; yet in the night, and alone, they have doubtful thoughts about it.

God never wrought a miracle to convince atheism, because his ordinary works convince it. *Bacon.*

Nothing is so important to any man, as his own state and condition: nothing so amazing as eternity. If therefore we find persons indifferent to the loss of their being, and to the danger of endless misery; it is impossible that this temper should be natural. *Pascal.*

If men understand not the evidence of religion, the more shame it is for them; but then immediately to leap out of ignorance into atheism is first to play the fool, and then run stark mad upon it. *Scott.*

It is a certain maxim, that such persons as take themselves out of God's protection are always at a loss, and know not how to dispose of themselves.

There is not a more ridiculous animal than an atheist, in his retirement. *Spec.*

M 2 *Cicero*

Cicero has obferved, that no kind of men are more afraid of GOD, than fuch as pretend not to believe his being. Thefe are the men who above all others are moft liable to be affected with dread and trembling, more efpecially in the time of ficknefs, and the approaches of death.

While we are in this life, our beft and fecureft condition is expofed to a world of fad and uncomfortable accidents, which we have neither the wifdom to forefee, nor the power to prevent: and where fhall we find relief, if there be no GOD?

Superftition renders a man a fool, and fcepticifm makes him mad.

We have a thing called reafon within us, which is very ingenious in giving ftings to our miferies, and vexing us with cutting reflections upon them; but is not able to qualify one grief, or minifter the leaft of any folid comfort to us. *Scott.*

No man living can find where the depth of reafon lies, in denying every thing, and proving nothing; in queftioning the truth of firft principles, and bidding defiance to the common fenfe of all mankind. *Trapp.*

As the irrefolute man can never perform
any

any action well, ſo he that is not reſolved in religion, can be reſolved in nothing elſe.

Whoever believes himſelf free from the obligations of divine precepts, cannot look on himſelf as bound by any human laws.

To play with important truths, to diſturb the repoſe of eſtabliſhed tenets, to ſubtilize objections, and elude proof, is too often the ſport of youthful vanity, of which maturer experience commonly repents. There is a time when every man is weary of raiſing difficulties only to taſk himſelf with the ſolution, and deſires to enjoy truth, without the labour, or hazard of conteſt. *Johnſon.*

To make up a confirmed atheiſt, there muſt be a continued ſeries of the moſt reſolute oppoſition to all ſound reaſon, conſcience, conſideration, and all degrees of moral virtue, with whatſoever elſe illuſtrates the true dignity of our nature.

The impoſſibility of proving there is no God, is a demonſtration that there is one.

Though hell is generally acknowledged both as the fountain and receptacle of all wickedneſs; yet ſo great a monſter as ſpeculative atheiſm never was, nor will be found there.

M 3

If

If knowledge without religion were highly valuable, nothing would be more so, than the devil.

There is an axiom, evident by the very light of nature, *That* GOD *will reward every man according to his works in this life.* That there are future rewards and punishments, is a doctrine universally assented to by all nations and religions; and there is not any first principle in philosophy, in which mankind are more generally agreed.

Scepticism, and a resolute doubting, after sufficient evidence, is a greater enemy to philosophy, and true knowledge, than incredulity itself; the latter of which may crowd in some falsehoods; but the former will never suffer us to acknowledge any truth.

Licentiousness in opinion always makes way for licentiousness in practice.

When a man jests upon religion, or declares it is indifferent what religion we are of, it is most certain, that himself is of no religion at all.

Lord *Bacon*, toward the latter end of his life, said, that a little smattering in philosophy would lead a man to atheism; but a thorough insight into it will lead a man

back

back again to a firft caufe; and that the firft principle of right reafon is religion: and ferioufly profeffed, that, after all his ftudies and inquifitions, he durft not die with any other thoughts than thofe religion taught as it is profeffed among the chriftians.

There are few things reafon can difcover with fo much certainty and eafe, as its own infufficiency: thofe who are ignorant of this imperfection, are the greateft proofs of it. *Col.*

We have heard of fome particular men that have been reputed atheifts; but never of any country, or fociety of men, that profeffed atheifm. The world in general was ever fo far from believing no GOD, that they were prone to believe many gods; and, from the infancy of it, that opinion grew, and increafed with it.

The *Egyptians* of old, though of all others the moft infamous for their multiplying of gods, yet did affert *one* maker and chief governor of the world, under whom they did fuppofe feveral fubordinate deities; who, as his deputies, did prefide over feveral parts of the univerfe. *Wilkins.*

M 4   The

The confent of all men, fays *Seneca*, is of very great weight with us. A mark that a thing is true, is, when it appears fo to all the world. Thus we conclude there is a divinity, becaufe all men believe it, there being no nations, how corrupt foever they be, which deny it.

It is certain there never was a man that faid, there was no GOD, but he wifhed it fiift.

I never had a fight of my foul (fays the emperor *Aurelius*) and yet I have a great value for it, becaufe it is difcoverable by its operations; and, by my conftant experience of the power of GOD, I have a proof of his being, and a reafon for my veneration.

As atheifin is in all refpects hateful, fo in this, that it deprives human nature of the means to exalt itfelf above human frailty. *Bacon.*

There never was any fuch thing fince the fall of man, as what fome call the religion of nature; that is, a religion without a Saviour. All that mercy and goodnefs, which GOD has ever fince the fall fhown to finners, in forgiving true penitents, and rewarding pious and virtuous men, is owing to this promife, and to the accomplifhment of it. *Sherlock.*

Natu-

Natural theology is, in itſelf, a poor weak thing; and reaſon unaſſiſted had not been able to carry the cleareſt philoſophers very far, in their purſuits after divine matters.   We have ſeen this in practical truths; and the reaſon lies ſtronger in ſuch as are ſpeculative. *Baker.*

A body of ethics, proved to be the law of nature, from principles of reaſon, and teaching all the duties of life, I think nobody will ſay the world had before our Saviour's time. *Locke.*

The men of reaſon, who think natural reaſon ſufficient for all the purpoſes of religion, reject all revelation, and conſequently all divine promiſes, which can be known only by revelation. *Sherlock.*

God has wiſely provided, in his preſent adminiſtration of things, to give us inſtances enough of his juſt procedure toward the good and bad; and yet to leave us inſtances enough of unrewarded virtue, and proſperous wickedneſs, to aſſure us he intends an after-reckoning. *Scott.*

There is this great miſchief always attending diſputes about religion, that, while our heads are ſo buſily employed in diſcuſſing its truth, our hearts are in danger of

M 5   loſing

lofing its power and efficacy. Many, from a denial of the *three perfons*, at laft advance to a denial of the *one* GOD. *Trapp.*

An intemperate curiofity, that rudely rufhes upon a facred myftery, without any reverence to its awful retirements, has done near as much mifchief to chriftianity, as infidelity itfelf.

It is obfervable, that the prefent deifts have not drawn and publifhed any fcheme of religion, or catalogue of the duties they are obliged to perform, or whence fuch obligations arife. They do not tell us, that they look on man as an accountable creature; nor, if they do, for what, and to whom, or when, that account is to be made, and what rewards and punifhments will attend it.

An atheift is got one point beyond the devils; for *they believe and tremble.*

How can we expeft to underftand the myfteries of Providence, fince we cannot underftand the works of nature.

As infidelity is the greateft fin, fo for GOD to give a man over to it is the greateft punifhment.

It is good counfel given to the *Athenians*, To be fure that king *Philip* was dead be-

before they expreſſed their joy at the report of it, leſt they might find him alive to revenge their haſly triumph. The like advice may be proper to all unbelievers: let them be ſure there is no GOD, before they preſume to defy him, leſt they find him at laſt to aſſert his being to their deſtruction.

Impenitency is the undoubted iſſue of incredulity.

I ſhould think it much more eaſy and rational (ſays lord *Bacon*) to believe all the fables in the poets, the Legend, the Talmud, and the Alccran, than that this univerſal frame ſhould be without a Creator and Governor.

All philoſophers agree, that though matter itſelf is changed into a thouſand different ſhapes, yet not any one particle of it utterly periſhes: much leſs can we think, that GOD deſtroys any principle of life, which he has made by nature immortal. *Sherlcck.*

He that walks only by the light of nature, walks in darkneſs.

The learned earl of *Northampton*, being troubled with atheiſtical ſuggeſtions, put them all off this way, *viz.* If I could give any account how myſelf, or any thing elſe, had a being without God ; how there came fo uniform and fo conftant a confent of mankind, of all ages, tempers, and educations (otherwife differing fo much in their apprehenfions) about the being of God, the immortality of the foul, and religion ; in which they could not likely either deceive fo many, or, being fo many, could not be deceived, I could be an atheift.

Nothing has more horror than annihilation. The worft that good men can fear is the beft that evil can wifh for; which is the diffolution of the foul in death. *Card.*

It has been rightly obferved, that in one point the atheift is the moft credulous man in the world, who believes the univerfe to be the production of chance.

When an atheift difputes with a chriftian againft Providence, if he will fay any thing to the purpofe, he muft difpute againft Providence upon the fuppofition of another life; and prove, that the eternal rewards and punifhments of the next world cannot vindicate the wifdom and juftice of Providence in this. This is the true ftate of the controverfy : bring them to this iffue, and they will find little to fay, which will give any trouble to a wife man to anfwer. *Sherlock.*

They

They that deny a GOD, deftroy man's nobility; for certainly man is of kin to the beafts by his body; and, if he be not of kin to GOD by his fpirit, he is an ignoble creature. *Bacon.*

They have gained a great prize indeed (fays *Cicero*) who have perfuaded themfelves to believe, that, when death comes, they fhall utterly perifh! What comfort is there, what is there to be boafted of, in that opinion? If in this I err, that I think the fouls of men immortal, I err with pleafure; nor will I ever, while I live, be forced out of an opinion which yields me fo much delight.

The foundations of all religion lie in two things, that there is a GOD who rules the world, and that the fouls of men are capable of fubfifting after death: *For he that comes unto GOD, muft believe that he is, and that he is a rewarder of them that feek him.* So that, if thefe things be not fuppofed as moft agreeable to human reafon, we cannot imagine upon what grounds mankind fhould embrace any way of religion at all.

If the foul exifts not after death, all differtation concerning future felicity or infelicity muft be vain and abfurd. *Plato.*

Why

Why fhould God exercife fo much patience toward wicked men, and bear fo long with them, were it not in great goodnefs to give them time for repentance, that they may efcape eternal miferies? Why fhould he afflict good men all their lives, whofe virtues deferve a more profperous fortune, only to exercife their faith and patience, and to advance them ftill to more divine perfections; unlefs he intended to reward their prefent fufferings, and their eminent virtue, with a brighter and more glorious crown? *Sherlock.*

The riches of imagination are poor, and all the rivers of eloquence are dry, in fupplying thought on an infinite fubject.

That all temporal worldly bleffings are common both to good and bad, the *Stoics* faw: that this, if there were no more in it than fo, could not ftand with God's juftice and goodnefs (which to deny is to deny that there is a God) they faw likewife. Upon this ground *Plato*'s illation was, That after this life there muft needs be a judgment, when both good and bad fhall according to their deeds be rewarded.

As practical, fo fpeculative wickednefs has ufually another afpect, when it ftands in the

the shadow of death, than in the dazzling beams of health and vigour.

The learned Mr. *Selden*, not long before he died, sent for Bp. *Usher* and Dr. *Langbain*, and discoursed to them to this purpose : that he had surveyed most parts of learning, yet could not recollect any passage out of those infinite books and manuscripts he was master of, wherein he could rest his soul, save of the *Holy Scriptures*.

All sorts of men that have gone before us into an eternal state, have left this great observation behind them : from experience they have found, that what vain thoughts soever men may, in the heat of their youth, entertain of *religion*, they will sooner or later, feel a testimony GOD has given it in every man's breast, which will one day make them serious, either by the inexpressible fears, terrors, and agonies of a troubled mind, or the inconceivable peace, comfort, and joy of a good conscience.

The zeal of spreading atheism is, if possible, more absurd than atheism itself. The truth of it is, the greatest number of this set of men are those, who, for want of a virtuous education, or examining the grounds of religion, know so very little of the matter,

ter, that their infidelity is but another term for their ignorance. *Spec.*

St. *Paul* tells us, that the gospel of our *Saviour* contains the last and great confirmation of another life; for *he hath brought life and immortality to light by the gospel.* And this is the only sure foundation of our hopes: we want no other arguments but this; and it seems as impertinent and superfluous to use them, as it would be to prove that by reason, which we know by sense; or to insist on some probabilities and moral arguments, when we can demonstrate. *Sherlock.*

It is no diminishing to revelation, that reason gives its suffrage too to the truths revelation has discovered. But it is our mistake to think, that because reason confirms them to us, we had the first certain knowledge of them from thence, and in that clear evidence we now possess them. *Locke.*

If we believe that GOD *is,* and act consonantly, we shall be *safe,* if he be *not*; and eternally *happy,* if he *be*: whereas if we believe, that he is *not,* we are sure to be *miserable* for ever, if he *be*; and are only *safe,* from being miserable for ever, if he be *not. Scott.*

What

What is this life but a circulation of little mean actions? We lie down and rife again, drefs and undrefs, feed and wax hungry, work, or play, and are weary, and then we lie down again, and the circle returns. We fpend the day in trifles, and, when the night comes, we throw ourfelves into the bed of folly, among dreams, and broken thoughts, and wild imaginations. Our reafon lies afleep by us, and we are, for the time, as errant brutes as thofe that fleep in the ftalls, or in the fields. Are not the capacities of man higher than thefe? And ought not his ambition and expectation to be greater? Let us be adventurers for another world; it is at leaft a fair and noble chance; and there is nothing in this worth our thoughts, or our paffions. If we fhould be difappointed, we are ftill no worfe than the reft of our expectations, we are eternally happy. *Bur.*

R L-

REFLECTIONS, MORAL and DIVINE.

DISCOURSES of morality, and reflections upon human nature, are the
beft means we can make ufe of to improve
our minds, and gain a true knowledge of
ourfelves; and confequently to recover our
fouls out of the vice, ignorance, and prejudice, which naturally cleave to them.
Spec.

The firft confideration a wife man fixes
upon, is the great end of his creation;
what it is, and wherein it confifts: the next
is, of the moft proper means to that end.

There is nothing which favours and falls
in with the natural greatnefs and dignity of
human nature, fo much as religion; which
does not only promife the intire refinement
of the mind, but the glorifying of the body
and the immortality of both. *Tat.*

There are no principles but thofe of religion to be depended on in cafes of real
diftrefs; and thefe are able to encounter the
worft emergencies, and to bear us up, under all the changes and chances to which
our life is fubject. *Sterne.*

If

If you would improve in wisdom, says *Epictetus*, you must be content to be thought foolish for neglecting the things of the world.

He that makes any thing his chiefest good, wherein virtue, reason, and humanity, do not bear a part, can never do the offices of friendship, justice, or liberality. *Cicero.*

Wisdom allows nothing to be good, that will not be so for ever; no man to be happy, but he that needs no other happiness than what he has within himself; no man to be great or powerful, that is not master of himself. *Seneca.*

Every state and condition of life, if attended with virtue, is undisturbed and delightful; but, when vice is intermixed, it renders even things that appear splendid, sumptuous, and magnificent, distasteful and uneasy to the possessor. *Plut.*

Religion is nothing else but the knowledge of the most excellent truths, the contemplation of the most glorious objects, and the hope of the most ravishing pleasures; and the practice of such duties as are most serviceable to our happiness, and to our peace, our health, our honour, our prosperity, and our eternal welfare.

Vir-

Virtue is like precious odours, moſt fragrant by being cruſhed: for proſperity beſt diſcovers vice; but adverſity beſt diſcovers virtue. *Bacon.*

The chiefeſt properties of wiſdom, are, to be mindful of things paſt, careful for things preſent, and provident for things to come. *Raleigh.*

When a man has once got a habit of virtue, all his actions are equal.

The firſt ſtep toward virtue is to abſtain from vice. No man has true ſound ſenſe, who is immoral. *Spec.*

Omiſſion of good is a commiſſion of evil.

A good man is influenced by GOD himſelf, and has a kind of divinity within him. *Seneca.*

Virtue needs no outward pomp; her very countenance is ſo full of majeſty, that the proudeſt pay her reſpect, and the profaneſt are awed by her preſence.

It is a great diſgrace to religion to imagine, that it is an enemy to mirth and cheerfulneſs, and a ſevere exactor of penſive looks and ſolemn faces. *Scott.*

All

All virtues are in agreement: all vices are at variance. *Sen.*

Were there but one virtuous man in the world, he would hold up his head with confidence and honour; he would fhame the world, and not the world him. *South.*

Any fin, committed in jeft, is greater than when it is done in earneft.

Though it be a truth very little received, that virtue is its own reward; it is furely an undeniable one, that vice is its own punifhment.

Whoever confiders the ftate and condition of human nature, and upon this view, how much ftronger the natural motives are to virtue than to vice, would expect to find the world much better than it is, or ever has been; for who would fuppofe the generality of mankind to betray fo much folly, as to act againft the common intereft of their own kind, as every man does who yields to the temptation of what is wrong. *Sterne.*

The fum of chriftianity or morality is, *Give and forgive; bear and forbear.*

If a man would but confult this golden rule *of dealing as he would be dealt by;* thofe
very

very paffions, which incline him to *wrong* others, would inftruct him to *right* them.

He who makes an idol of his interest, makes a martyr of his integrity.

It is ufually feen, that the wifer men are about the things of this world, the lefs wife they are about the things of the next. *Gilfon.*

The principal point of wifdom is, to know how to value things juft as they deferve. There is nothing in the world worth being a knave for.

He who increafes the endearment of life, increafes at the fame time the terrors of death. *Tcung.*

The neglecting of the ftudy of true wifdom, will revenge itfelf; the defpifers of it not being able to do well in their greateft profperity, and the lovers of it not doing ill in their loweft adverfities.

If you take pains in what is good, the pains vanifh, the good remains; if you take pleafure in what is evil, the evil remains, and the pleafure vanifhes. What are you the worfe for pains, or the better for pleafure, when both are paft?

Virtue commands good mens refpect, and all mens honour; and banifhes every

kind

kind of deformity from the perfon in whom it refides.

Though a great man precede us by reafon of his dignity, we may go before him in the way of perfection.

It is infolent, as well as unnatural, to trample upon the venerable decays of human nature: he that acts in this manner, does but expofe his own future condition, and laughs at himfelf beforehand. *Spec.*

The true fpirit of religion cheers as well as compofes the foul: it is not the bufinefs of virtue to extirpate the affections of the mind, but to regulate them. *Spec.*

The difeafes of the body are better difcovered, when they increafe; but the difeafes of the foul grow more obfcure, and the moft fick are the lefs fenfible. *Seneca.*

Human frailty is no excufe for criminal immorality.

Every man, committing a trefpafs, is the prifoner of juftice, as foon as he has done it. *Plut.*

As many as are the difficulties which virtue has to encounter in this world, her force is yet fuperior. *Shaftefb.*

Nobody giving attention to *Diogenes*, while he difcourfed of virtue, he fell a finging; and every one crowding to hear him, he cried out, Great gods! how much more is folly admired than wifdom.

Nothing is more ridiculous than to be ferious about trifles, and to be trifling about ferious matters.

The total lofs of reafon is lefs deplorable than the total depravation of it. *Cowl.*

Wifdom and virtue make the poor rich, and the rich honorable.

Virtue is a fteady principle, and gives ftability to every thing elfe; though, while good men live in a giddy and rolling world, they muft, in fome meafure, feel its uncertain motions. *Sherlock.*

Religion is the beft armour in the world, but the worft cloak.

The hypocrite is never fo far from being a good chriftian, as when he looks likeft one.

All earthly delights are fweeter in the expectation than the enjoyment; all fpiritual pleafures more in fruition than expectation.

The days of pleafure are often the vigils of repentance. *Gracian.*

The

The defire of power in excefs caufed the angels to fall; the defire of knowledge in excefs caufed man to fall; but in charity there is no excefs. *Bacon.*

Charity makes the beft conftitution of things and perfons, excufes weaknefs, extenuates mifcarriages, makes the beft of every thing, forgives every body, and ferves all.

It fares with men of an evil confcience, when they muft die, as it doth with riotous fpendthrifts, when they muft pay their debts: they will not come to an account, for the diftruft they have of their ability to fatisfy for what they have done. *Richl.*

There is hardly any wicked man, but when his own cafe is reprefented to him under the perfon of another, will freely enough pafs fentence againft the wickednefs he himfelf is guilty of.

The *Arabians* have a faying, It is not good to jeft with God, death, or the devil: for the firft neither can nor will be mocked; the fecond mocks all men one time or another; and the third puts an eternal farcafm on thofe that are too familiar with him.

One

One of the greateſt artifices the devil uſes to engage men in vice and debauchery is, to faſten names of contempt on certain virtues; and to fill weak ſouls with a fooliſh fear of paſſing for ſcrupulous, ſhould they deſire to put them in practice. *Paſcal.*

It is ſaid of *Socrates*, Whether he is teaching the rules of an exact morality, whether he is anſwering his corrupt judges, whether he is receiving ſentence of death, or ſwallowing the poiſon, he is ſtill the ſame man; that is to ſay, calm, quiet, undiſturbed, intrepid; in a word, wiſe to the laſt.

When a man has got ſuch a great and exalted ſoul, as that he can look upon life and death, riches and poverty, with indifference; and cloſely adheres to honeſty, in whatever ſhape ſhe preſents herſelf, then it is, that virtue appears with ſuch a brightneſs, as that all the world muſt admire her beauties. *Cicero.*

Where there is no conflict, there can be no conqueſt; where there is no conqueſt, there is no crown.

In human life there is a conſtant change of fortune; and it is unreaſonable to expect an exemption from the common fate: life

it-

itfelf decays, and all things are daily on the change. *Plut.*

Trouble marches before virtue, and after vice; but pleafure follows virtue, and vice is followed by repentance.

To love the public, to ftudy univerfal good, and to promote the intereft of the whole world, as far as lies within our power, is the height of goodnefs, and makes that temper which we call divine. *Shaftefb.*

A firm faith, and true honefty, are not to be forced by neceffity, or corrupted by reward.

A little wrong, done to another, is a great injury done to ourfelves. The fevereft punifhment of an injury is the confcience of having done it; and no man fuffers more than he that is turned over to the pain of repentance.

When we act according to our duty, we commit the event to him by whofe laws our actions are governed, and who will fuffer none to be finally punifhed for obedience. But when in profpect of fome good, whether natural or moral, we break the rules prefcribed to us, we withdraw from the direction of fuperior wifdom, and take all confequences upon ourfelves. *Johnfon.*

It

It cofts us more to be miferable, than would make us perfectly happy. How cheap and eafy to us is the fervice of virtue, and how dear do we pay for our vices!

The feeds of all the virtues are implanted in us with the firft ftamina of our frame.

We may be as good as we pleafe, if we pleafe to be good. *Barrow.*

We can ftrike up bargains, and make contracts, by proxy; but all men muft work out their falvation in perfon.

No man fhould be confident of his own merit; for the beft err: neither fhould any rely too much upon his own judgment; for the wifeft are deceived.

Nothing can give us fo juft a notion of the depravity of mankind in general, as an exact knowledge of our own corruptions in particular.

A virtuous man may be innocently re-venged of his enemies, by perfifting in well-doing; and a wicked man, by reforming his life.

Moft men are afraid of a bad name; but few fear their confciences. *Pliny.*

No man ever offended his own con-fcience, but firft or laft it was revenged upon him for it. *South.*

6   It

It was an admirable saying of *Plutarch*, That a city may as well be built in the air, as a commonwealth or kingdom be either constituted or conserved without the support of religion.

Alexander Severus allowed christianity out of love to this one precept, *Do not that to another, which thou wouldst not have done to thyself.*

It is a miserable folly to be wise in wickedness.

The more a man presumes, the greater reason he has to fear.

The fear of hell does a great deal toward the keeping of us in our way to heaven; and if it were not for the penalty, the laws neither of GOD, nor of man, would be obeyed. *L'Estr.*

Heaven's gate is strait, but not shut up; though but few enter, all may.

We ought to think ourselves very happy, in that we know enough to make us happy. If we are not so happy as we desie, it is well we are not so miserable as we deserve. There are none but have received more good than they have done, and done more evil than they have suffered.

Divine

Divine meditations do not only in power subdue all sensual pleasures, but also far exceed them in sweetness and delight. *Bacon.*

To be furious in religion is to be irreligiously religious. Persecution can be no argument to persuade, nor violence the way to conversion.

The *Mexicans* salute their new-born infants in this manner: *Child, thou art come into the world to suffer: endure, and hold thy peace.*

Were angels, if they look into the ways of men, to give in their catalogue of worthies, how different would it be from that which any of our own species would draw up! We are dazzled with the splendor of titles, the ostentation of learning, the noise of victories: they, on the contrary, see the philosopher in the cottage, who possesses his soul in patience and thankfulness, under the pressures of what little minds call poverty and distress. The evening's walk of a wise man is more illustrious in their sight, than the march of a general at the head of a hundred thousand men. A contemplation of God's works, a generous concern for the good of mankind, and un-

unfeigned exercise of humility, only denominate men great and glorious. *Addif.*

Several who have tasted all the pleasures of sin, forsake it, and come over to virtue: but there is scarce an instance to be found of any that had well experimented the delights of virtue, that ever could be drawn off from it, or find in his heart to fall back to his former course.

Virtue has so sweet a power, that every one will wear her livery, though few do her service.

The first of all virtues is innocence; the next is modesty. If we banish modesty out of the world, she carries away with her half the virtue that is in it. *Spec.*

All our wisdom and happiness consists summarly in the knowledge of GOD, and ourselves. To know, and to do, is the compendium of our duty.

To do evil for evil is human corruption; to do good for good is civil retribution; but to do good for evil is christian perfection.

A peaceful conscience, honest thoughts, virtuous actions, and an indifference for casual events, are blessings without end or

mea-

meafure. This confummated ftate of felicity is only a fubmiffion to the dictate of right nature: the foundation of it is wifdom and virtue; the knowledge of what we ought to do, and the conformity of the will to that knowledge. *Sen.*

Sir *W. Raleigh*, difcourfing with fome friends in the Tower, of happinefs, urged, that it was not only a freedom from difeafes and pains of the body, but from anxiety and vexation of fpirit; not only to enjoy the pleafures of fenfe, but peace of confcience, and inward tranquillity: and this happinefs, fo fuitable to the immortality of our fouls, and the eternal ftate we muft live in, is only to be met with in religion.

What can be more fuitable to a rational creature, than to employ reafon to contemplate that divine Being, which is both the author of its reafon, and nobleft object about which it can poffibly be employed? *Boyle.*

How is it poffible, that mankind, which toils out a weary life in eager purfuits of every appearance of good, fhould forget that which we confefs the fupreme? *Young.*

We have a great work on our hands: the gofpel promifes to believe; the commands to obey; temptations to refift; paffions

fions to conquer. And this muft be done, or we are undone.

Religion is exalted reafon, refined from the groffer parts of it: it is both the foundation and crown of all virtues: it is morality improved, and raifed to its height, by being carried nearer heaven, the only place where perfection refides. *Halifax.*

A firm faith is the beft divinity, good life the beft philofophy, a clear confcience the beft law, honefty the beft policy, and temperance the beft phyfic.

Every virtue gives a man a degree of felicity in fome kind: honefty gives a man a good report; juftice, eftimation; prudence, refpeét; courtefy and liberality, affeétion; temperance gives health; fortitude, a quiet mind, not to be moved by any adverfity. *Walfingham.*

Virtue is a bleffing which man alone poffeffes, and no other creature has any title to but himfelf. All is nothing without her, and fhe alone is all. The other bleffings of this life are oftentimes imaginary: fhe is always real. She is the foul of the foul, the life of life, and crown of all perfeétions. If mortal excellence be worthy of our defires, fure the eternal ought to be the objeét of our ambition. *Gracian.*

Of

Of DEATH and ETERNITY.

THERE is not a more effectual way to revive the true spirit of christianity than seriously to meditate on what we commonly call the four last things; death, judgment, heaven, and hell. *Sherlock.*

Destiny has decreed all men to die; but to die well is the particular privilege of the virtuous and good.

To die is the fate of man; but to die with lingering anguish, is generally his folly. *Johnson.*

Our decays are as much the work of nature, as the first principles of our being. We die as fast as we live. Every moment subtracts from our duration on earth, as much as it adds to it.

As there is no covenant to be made with death, so no agreement for the arrest and stay of time: it keeps its pace, whether we redeem and use it well, or no.

If we would reason right, and compute upon the notion of eternity, we should not be much concerned, whether our life was

to

to end on the morrow, or a thousand years hence. *Antoninus.*

He that has given God his worship, and man his due, is entertained with comfortable presages, wears off smoothly, and expires in pleasure. *Plato.*

Death is no more than a turning us over from time to eternity. It leads to immortality; and that is recompence enough for suffering of it.

A little while is enough to view the world in. Nature treads in a circle, and has much the same face through the whole course of eternity. Live well, and make virtue thy guide; and then let death come sooner or later, it matters not.

The way to bring ourselves with ease to a contempt of the world, is to think daily of leaving it.

To neglect at any time preparation for death, is to sleep on our post at a siege; but to omit it in old age, is to sleep at an attack. *Johnson.*

Few take care to live well, but many to live long; though it is in a man's power to do the former, but in no man's power to do the latter.

N 6 The

The caſt of mind, which is natural to a wiſe man, makes him look forward into futurity, and conſider what will be his condition millions of ages hence, as well as what it is at preſent. *Spec.*

There is nothing, which muſt end, to be valued for its continuance.

He that dies well has lived long enough. Soon as death enters upon the ſtage, the tragedy of life is done.

There are a great many miſeries, which nothing but death can give relief to. This puts an end to the ſorrows of the afflicted and oppreſſed: it ſets the priſoners at liberty; it dries up the tears of the widows and fatherleſs; it eaſes the complaints of the hungry and naked; it tames the proudeſt tyrants, and puts an end to all our labours. And the contemplation on it ſupports men under their preſent adverſities, eſpecially when they have a proſpect of a better life after this. *Sherlock.*

To live is a gift; to die is a debt. This life is only a prelude to eternity. *Sen.*

It is the perfection of happineſs, neither to wiſh for death nor to fear it.

Men

Men take more pains for this world, than heaven would coſt them; and, when they have what they aim at, do not live to enjoy it. The grave lies unſeen between us and the object which we reach after: where one lives to enjoy whatever he has in view, ten thouſand are cut off in the purſuit of it. *Spec.*

All our knowledge, our employments, our riches, and our honours, muſt end in death; ſo that we muſt ſeek a ſanctuary of happineſs ſomewhere elſe. *St Evr.*

It is an excellent proof of wiſdom, frequently to meditate on the eternity of our worthieſt part, and to conſider, that this compact of the elements muſt ſoon ſuffer a diſſolution. Beauty is a flower which ſoon withers; health changes, and ſtrength abates; but innocency is immortal, and a comfort both in life and death.

When *Socrates* was told by a friend, that his judges had ſentenced him to death: *And has not nature,* ſaid he, *paſſed the ſame ſentence upon them?*

It is good every night to caſt up our accounts, and repent for the miſdeeds of that day; then, our ſins being dead before ourſelves, we ſhall have nothing elſe to do at the hour of our death, but to die.

How

How irrational is a late repentance! Muft the body be befieged with ficknefs, before that work be done, on which eternal life depends?

The greateft wifdom is to keep our eye perpetually on a future judgment, for the direction and government of our lives; which will furnifh us with fuch principles of action, as cannot be fo well learned any other way. *Sherlock.*

They who continually think of death are the only perfons that do not fear it. *Plato.*

How miferable is that man, that cannot look backward, but with fhame, nor forward, without terror! What comfort will his riches afford him in his extremity; or what will all his fenfual pleafures, his vain and empty titles, robes, dignities, and crowns, avail him in the day of his diftrefs?

The time is near, when the great and the rich muft leave his land and his well-built houfe; and of all the trees of his orchards and woods, nothing fhall attend him to his grave, but oak for his coffin, and cyprefs for his funeral. *Taylor.*

None

None are greater wafters than thofe that build coftly monuments for the dead. A man were better forgotten, who has nothing of greater moment to regifter his name by than a tomb.

Pofthumous fame has little more in it, than filence and obfcurity.

The humour of *Tiberius* is ridiculous, yet common; who was more folicitous to extend his renown to pofterity, than to render himfelf acceptable to men of his own time.

He that is folicitous about being talked of when he is dead, fhould confider, that all his admirers will quickly be gone; and what is their panegyric, or his fine monument to him that knows nothing of the matter? *Antoninus.*

Pompous funerals, and fumptous monuments, are made more out of a defign to gratify the vanity of the living, than to do honour to the dead. Greatnefs may build the tomb; but it is goodnefs muft make the epitaph.

He that is your chief mourner, will quickly want another for himfelf.

When

When death has once made a diffolution of the parts that compofe us, there is fo little room required to contain them, that it is even ridiculous to be concerned about it. Time, which preys upon nature itfelf, will at length confume our tomb, though it were of adamant or brafs.

How many famous men are dropt out of hiftory, and forgotten! And how many poets and panegyrifts, that promifed to keep up other people's names, have loft their own! *Antoninus*.

At my death (fays fir *T. Brown*) I mean to take a total adieu of the world, not caring for a monument, hiftory, or epitaph, not fo much as the memory of my name to be found any where, but in the univerfal regifter of GOD.

In the grave there is no diftinction of perfons; which made *Diogenes* fay, when fearching a charnel houfe, That he could find no difference between the fkull of king *Philip*, and another man's.

Under the gofpel, GOD is pleafed with a living facrifice; but the offerings of the dead, fuch as teftamentary charities are, which are intended to have no effect fo long as we live, are no better than dead facrifices;

fices; and it may be queſtioned, whether they will be brought into the account of our lives, if we do no good while we are living. Theſe deathbed charities are too like a deathbed repentance: men ſeem to give their eſtates to GOD and the poor, juſt as they part from their ſins, when they can keep them no longer. *Sherlock.*

What are honours, fame, wealth, and power, when compared with the expectation of a being without end, and a happineſs adequate to that end? How poor will theſe things ſeem at our laſt hour! And how joyful will that man be, who has led a honeſt virtuous life, and travelled to heaven, though through the rougheſt ways of poverty, affliction, and contempt!

Good men are happy both in life and death; the wicked in neither.

The young may die ſhortly; but the aged cannot live long: green fruit may be plucked off, or ſhaken down; but the ripe will fall of itſelf.

A gentleman, upon his deathbed, laid this one command upon his wild ſon, *That he ſhould every day of his life be one hour a-lone:* which he conſtantly obſerved; and, thereby growing ſerious, became a new man. The

The time, and manner, and circumstances of every particular man's death, are not determined by an abfolute and unconditional decree: for what place can there be for conditional promifes, where an abfolute decree is paft? How can any man be faid not to live out half his days, if he lives as long as GOD has decreed he fhall live. *Sherlock.*

A holy defire of a religious death is not the humour, the fancy, the fear of fome men, but the ferious wifh of all. Many have lived wickedly; very few, in their fenfes, died fo.

As a good conclufion is a honour to our whole life, fo an ill one cafts back infamy, and fullies all that went before.

There is nothing in hiftory that is fo improving to the reader, as thofe accounts which we meet with of the deaths of eminent perfons, and their behaviour in that dreadful feafon.

The great philofopher *Socrates*, on the day of his execution, a little before the draught of poifon was brought to him, entertaining his friends with a difcourfe on the immortality of the foul, faid, Whether or no GOD will approve of my actions, I know not; but this I am fure of, that I

have

have at all times made it my endeavour to pleafe him; and I have a good hope, that this my endeavour will be accepted by him.

Philip III, king of Spain, ferioufly reflecting upon the life he had led in the world, cried out upon his deathbed, Ah! how happy were I, had I fpent thofe twenty-three years that I have held my kingdom, in a retirement! Saying to his confeffor, My concern is for my foul, not my body.

Cardinal *Wolfey*, one of the greateft minifters of ftate that ever was, poured forth his foul in thefe fad words: Had I been as diligent to ferve my GOD, as I have been to pleafe my king, he would not have forfaken me now in my gray hairs.

Cardinal *Richlieu*, after he had given law to all Europe many years together, confeffed to P. *du Moulin*, that, being forced upon many irregularities in his lifetime, by that which they call reafon of ftate, he could not tell how to fatisfy his confcience upon feveral accounts. And, being afked one day by a friend, Why he was fo fad? he anfwered, The foul is a ferious thing; it muft be either fad here for a moment, or be fad for ever.

Cardi-

Cardinal *Mazarine*, having made religion wholly fubfervient to the fecular interefts, difcourfing one day with a Sorbon doctor concerning the immortality of the foul, and a man's eternal ftate, faid weeping; O my poor foul, whither wilt thou go? And afterward, feeing the queen-mother, faid to her, Madam, your favours undid me; and, were I to live my time again, I would be a capuchin, rather than a courtier.

Sir *John Mafon*, privy counfellor to king *Henry* VIII, &c. upon his deathbed, delivered himfelf to thofe about him, to this purpofe: I have feen five princes, and been privy counfellor to four. I have feen the moft remarkable obfervations in foreign parts, and been prefent at moft ftate tranf-actions for thirty years together; and have learned this after fo many years experience, that ferioufnefs is the greateft wifdom, temperance the beft phyfic, and a good confcience the beft eftate. Were I to live again, I would change the court for a cloifter, my privy counfellor's buftles for a hermit's retirement, and the whole life I lived in the palace, for one hour's enjoyment of God in the chapel: all things elfe forfake me befide my God, my duty, and my prayer.

Sir

Sir *Thomas Smith*, fecretary of ftate to queen *Elifabeth*, a quarter of a year before he died, fent to his friends, the bifhops of *Winchefte* and *Worcefter*, entreating them to draw him, out of the word of God, the plaineft and exacteft way of making his peace with him; adding, that it was great pity men knew not to what end they were born into this world, till they were ready to go out of it.

Sir *Philip Sidney* left this his laft farewell among his acquaintance: Govern your will and affections by the will and word of your Creator: in me behold the end of this world, and all its vanities.

Dr. *Donne*, a perfon of great parts and learning, being upon his deathbed, and taking his folemn farewell of his friends, faid; I repent of all my life, but that part of it I fpent in communion with God, and doing good.

In a letter which Mr. *Locke* wrote the year before his death, to one who had afked him this queftion, What is the fhorteft way to attain to a true knowledge of the chriftian religion in the full and juft extent of it? His anfwer is: Study the Holy Scriptures, efpecially the New Teftament;

therein

therein are contained the words of eternal life : it has GOD for its author, salvation for its end, and truth, without any mixture of error, for its matter.

In ancient time, the pope, at his inauguration, used to have four marble stones presented to him, out of which he chose one for his tomb-stone.

Cha les V, caused his own funeral to be celebrated, and for two years assisted at the prayers made on that occasion.

In order to our final doom and sentence, there needs but this one inquiry, Whether we were charitable, or uncharitable ? For a man who is possessed with a true divine charity, has all christian graces. A man who has not this divine principle, has no good in him; and that is enough to condemn him, without inquiring what evil he has done. *Sherlock.*

Great men, who are not animated with the spirit of religion, make the ceremony of their funeral the last refuge of their vanity. They endeavour to fix, to their memory, that which death is going to take from them; and gathering, as it were, the ruins of their glory in some pompous encomiums, stately mausoleums, and magnificent inscriptions, they make a kind

of

of charm of that funeral pomp, to remove from their minds, the mortifying image of their sad destiny.

Sir *W. Raleigh*, looking on the monument of princes, made this reflection: O just and mighty death! What none have dared, thou hast done; and whom all the world has flattered, thou alone has cast out of the world, and despised: thou hast drawn together all the far-stretched greatness, all the cruelty and ambition of man, and covered it all over with these two narrow words, *Hic jacet*.

The daring and bold sinners, who mocked at fear, especially at the fear of GOD, as a base unmanly passion; those mighty hectors, the great disturbers of mankind, will at the last day stand trembling before their Judge. On the other hand, with what triumph will good men lift up their heads; the poor and despised! their sorrows will then fly away like the shades of the night at the approach of the sun. *Sherlock.*

It is certainly necessary to retreat sometimes from company, and bar the door upon business and diversion; and, when we are thus disengaged, to inspect our practice, to state our accounts, and examine our conditions for eternity.

When

When I look upon the tombs of the great, every emotion of envy dies in me; when I read the epitaphs of the beautiful, every inordinate defire goes out; when I meet with the grief of parents upon a tomb-ftone, my heart melts with compaffion; when I fee the tomb of the parents them-felves, I confider the vanity of grieving for thofe whom we muft quickly follow; when I fee kings lying by thofe who de-pofed them; when I confider rival wits placed fide by fide, or the holy men that divided the world with their contefts and difputes, I reflect with forrow and afto-nifhment on the little competitions, fac-tions, and debates of mankind: when I read the feveral dates of the tombs, of fome that died as yefterday, and fome of fix hundred years ago, I confider that great day, when we fhall all of us be cotempo-raries, and make our appearance together. *Addifon.*

THE END.

www.ingramcontent.com/pod-product-compliance
Lightning Source LLC
Chambersburg PA
CBHW080549090426
42735CB00016B/3195